"I had a great time reading Jody's book on her time at Disney as I have been to many of the same places and events that she attended. She went well beyond recounting her experiences though, adding many layers of texture on the how and the why of Disney storytelling. Yet Jody knows the golden rule in this business: If you knew how the trick was done, it wouldn't be any fun anymore. At the end of the journey, she is simply in awe of the magic just as we all are, even today. Thank you, Jody, for taking us along on that journey."

—ROY P. DISNEY, grandnephew of Walt Disney

"Jody may be the most organized, focused person I've ever met, and she has excelled in every job she's held at the company. No one better embodies the Disney spirit."

—MICHAEL D. EISNER, former chairman and CEO of The Walt Disney Company

"If Mickey Mouse and Minnie Mouse had a baby, it would be Jody Dreyer."

—DICK COOK, former chairman, Walt Disney Studios

"I'm a huge believer in good storytelling. And as a fellow Disney fanatic I'm really excited to see the impact of this great read!"

—KATE VOEGELE, singer/songwriter, *One Tree Hill* actress and recording artist on *Disneymania 6*

"Jody Dreyer pulls the curtain back to reveal the inner workings of one of the most fascinating and successful companies on Earth. *Beyond the Castle* offers incredible insight for Disney fans and business professionals alike who will relish this peek inside the magic kingdom from Jody's unique perspective."

—DON HAHN, producer, *Beauty and the Beast*, *The Lion King*

BEYOND THE CASTLE

A GUIDE TO DISCOVERING YOUR HAPPILY EVER AFTER

JODY JEAN DREYER
WITH **STACY WINDAHL**

ZONDERVAN®

ZONDERVAN

Beyond the Castle
Copyright © 2017 by Jody J. Dreyer and Stacy Windahl

Requests for information should be addressed to:

Zondervan, *3900 Sparks Dr. SE, Grand Rapids, Michigan 49546*

ISBN 978-0-310-34705-7 (hardcover)

ISBN 978-0-310-35050-7 (audio)

ISBN 978-0-310-34725-5 (ebook)

Scripture quotations are taken from the Holy Bible, New International Version®, NIV®. Copyright © 1973, 1978, 1984, 2011 by Biblica, Inc.® Used by permission of Zondervan. All rights reserved worldwide. www.Zondervan.com. The "NIV" and "New International Version" are trademarks registered in the United States Patent and Trademark Office by Biblica, Inc.®

All photos, unless otherwise noted, are courtesy of the authors.

Any internet addresses (websites, blogs, etc.) and telephone numbers in this book are offered as a resource. They are not intended in any way to be or imply an endorsement by Zondervan, nor does Zondervan vouch for the content of these sites and numbers for the life of this book.

Cover design: Curt Diepenhorst
Cover illustration: Erwin Madrid
Interior design: Kait Lamphere
Interior imagery: © Mutanov Daniyar/Shutterstock, PhotoDisc

First printing July 2017 / Printed in the United States of America

APPLAUSE

To my Disney friends:
You are the heart and soul of the company,
the hardworking, magic-making, smile-giving
Disney cast members of yesterday, today, and
tomorrow. Each day you make dreams come
true. I am honored to have worked alongside
you and grateful to call you family.

CONTENTS

CASTLE NOTES

The conversations and events described in this book are retold from the author's best recollections and they are not written to represent word-for-word transcripts. Rather, the author has shared these personal stories in a way that evokes the feeling and meaning of what was said, and in all instances, the essence of the dialogue and attending circumstances is accurate. In addition, since The Walt Disney Company always has been and will continue to be a dynamic enterprise, the business practices described within this account were observed during the author's career but may have changed since.

Throughout this book, the author's Disney colleagues are mentioned by first names with last names in parentheses upon introduction in each chapter. Otherwise, it's first names only. Disney is a first-name company. For years, the author worked alongside cast members knowing details about their family or even a recent vacation without knowing their last names. Walt himself established the first name tradition believing that first names invited informality and enabled the flow of ideas. But if you feel the first name reference is a little unusual, we understand. Consider this encouragement from a Disney University training pamphlet entitled *Welcome to the Show*: "You may find our first name policy difficult at first: old habits are hard to break. But once you get the hang of it, we think you'll like our friendly, family way of doing things." We hope so, too.

FOREWORD

Happily *Ever After.* Can that really be true? Is there such a thing? It all seems so impossible. However, I must confess that having worked as a Disney animator on fairy tales for many years, I was particularly drawn to animating the characters who believe the impossible is indeed possible. Ariel, though a mermaid, falls in love with a prince who walks on two legs and breathes air! The Beast is determined to believe that Belle could somehow look past his ugly beastly exterior, tusks and all, and love him for who he is inside.

There is hope at work here . . . and faith . . . and love. Who doesn't want to believe in that?

Beyond the Castle: A Guide to Discovering Your Happily Ever After is a book about how the little things count in big ways. One might call them details, but they are what makes the difference.

Jody's formative years in the Midwest have left her with a homespun practicality that she expresses with her own Mark Twain wisdom. She sees the ups and downs of life from a Disneyland roller coaster perspective and says, "Without a hill, there's no thrill!" She divides the accumulation of a lifetime of stuff into "Treasure, Trash, and Trail Mix." She shares "Lessons learned from the opening of Euro Disneyland" and how to avoid the effect of "Queue Rage" in waiting lines.

I first met Jody when she was working for Disney CEO Michael Eisner as the head of Corporate Synergy. I was an artist and not used to chumming around with Disney executives. But Jody, in her own natural way, made me feel at ease and relaxed. She exemplified that welcoming, Disney quality. There is a certain "pixie dust" magic to her.

As I read Jody's words I find that same magic of belief in what she says . . . she lived it, loved it, and believed in it. Now she's sharing that with others.

This is above all a book of hope. The "castles" of our life are not always shiny spires reflecting the sunshine. Sometimes they become quite dark and in need of transformation.

I will never forget seeing Beast's castle for the first time. It was the fall of 1989 and our animation team for *Beauty and the Beast* was in France on a research trip. We were driving down a long narrow road through the woods in the Loire Valley to visit the famous royal chateau, Chambord. Through the early morning fog a dark shadowy form emerged with its spires, walls, and towers, as if the Beast himself was personified by the stone edifice. As we approached I imagined Beast running through its rooms filled with ancient furniture and draperies. But once having stepped inside I found its hallways empty, all its interior decorations long gone. Yet, somehow I could still feel the energy and life that once animated its halls. My imagination came alive and I could envision a chateau transformed into the fairytale castle at the end of *Beauty and the Beast*.

Castles can inspire magic—in stories, films, and beyond. Now, after a thirty-year career within Walt Disney's Magic Kingdoms, Jody transforms those years of experience into a fascinating story . . . fairytale castles, happy endings and all.

Glen Keane, Director/Animator, Disney Legend
April 2017

ONCE UPON A TIME
Every Life Can Be a Fairy Tale

My love of The Walt Disney Company started long before my internship in The Walt Disney World College Program, the first of my twenty-two positions in a thirty-year career at Disney. Perhaps it can be traced back to my earliest school years. My mom likes to tell the story of the time I organized my kindergarten class shoe by shoe. I had become frustrated with the confusion at the end of the school day as kids scrambled to find their shoes. The obvious solution was to put each kid's shoes in the same place each day. (Right?) While I don't recall much of this, apparently it made good sense to me at the time. Still does, actually. Another early indication of my Disney destiny was what I loved most about one of my favorite high school jobs, working for the American Automobile Association. I loved putting the maps in the right order and making sure that the office was set up to give proper directions to all the members that would come in over the busy weekend. All roads led to Disney, the number one vacation destination.

I guess it's no surprise that for the decades I worked at Disney, in one form or another, my jobs involved creating order out of chaos, finding hidden opportunities, encouraging everyone to work together, and putting plain old common sense to work for the good of the company.

And since you can't separate who you are from what you learn along the way, a little background might be helpful. My experiences have been shaped by the intersection of three themes in my life: my Midwest sensibilities, a predisposition to organization, and a love of (planned) spontaneity and celebration.

My dad was born and raised on an Indiana farm. My mom also called Indiana home and Mom and Dad both attended Purdue in the 1950s. She was a twirler in the Boilermaker All-American Marching Band, a big deal. Together they raised my three siblings and me in Ohio. That Midwest upbringing all but ensured my love of sports (with particular reverence for the Cubs and the Big Ten tradition).

My mom, Jacque, a majorette
in the Purdue All-American
Marching Band.

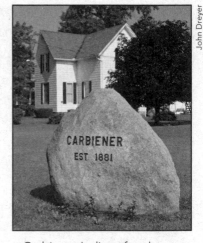

John Dreyer

Carbiener Indiana farmhouse
where Dad and his siblings
were born and raised.

It also ensured that I would choose simplicity and common sense over complexity and nuance, and that the family farm would be a touchstone throughout my life. The farm dispenses truth daily. It instructs on the immutable laws about sowing and reaping, proving that today is the parent of tomorrow. It teaches about working hard—and working together, often through adversity. I discovered that growing up in the heartland with the family farm in the backdrop was a straight path to Disney's Main Street, U.S.A.

Second, my mom is a neat freak with a genetic tendency toward order. Her penchant aligned well with my dad's Navy ROTC training and service. Needless to say, I grew up knowing that a squared-away, tip-top, shipshape existence beats a chaotic one, and that order requires a practiced plan. Such a part of my childhood, this became my nature. But I don't want to give you the wrong idea here. My family is crazy fun and, as we like to say, if no one gets hurt and it's legal, go for it!

Dad, Wayne, a shipshape Navy man.

My cowriter, Stacy, with sister Chris and their worn-out dad on the first of many Disney World visits.

Which leads me to a third theme. I have realized that because we had a plan, our family could party. Good times were a part of the program. (Just check the schedule. Fun and spontaneity were in there.) I love a good celebration. And why not? We too often carry our lives with its duties and obligations like a burdensome sack on our backs when those very duties and obligations can actually be a gift we're meant to wrap our arms around.

Last—and what supersedes everything else—I love God and I read the Bible. I want to live out my faith in every part of my life. But this is not a Bible study. It's a story. Just my story.

Now about my partner in this work—another intersection. I met Stacy several years ago through our deep affection for Young Life, a ministry created to love on kids. Both of us met Young Life when we were in high school—both in Ohio. In our experience, Young Life, like Disney, practices gracious hospitality and aims to surprise and delight. And Young Life and Disney genuinely like kids and care about the happily ever after of each one they meet. Stacy has been a storyteller for Young Life for sixteen years. As a freelance writer, she has written stories of Young Life leaders and kids in magazine articles, and she has contributed to books, brochures, and all kinds of Young Life communications. Since we share a passion for faith, family, and fairy tales, it's no wonder the two of us struck up a friendship that has resulted in this writing project. It was fitting that we celebrated Young Life's seventy-fifth birthday together with five thousand Young Life friends watching a fireworks extravaganza at Walt Disney World. Some things are meant to be.

We invite you to come with us to discover some things you might not know about Disney—including the man himself. For example, I wonder if you knew . . .

- Walt grew up in the Midwest, and Disneyland's Main Street, U.S.A. is reminiscent of his boyhood home in Marceline, Missouri.
- Walt's family also lived on a farm for a time and he said those were among his fondest memories.
- Walt tried to enlist in the armed forces in 1918. He was rejected because of his young age—sixteen. Undaunted, he volunteered with the Red Cross, traveled overseas, and drove an ambulance. His ambulance wasn't discreetly camouflaged, but instead was covered with his drawings and cartoons.
- Walt's early experiences, travels, and adventures became the foundation for the iconic enterprise that bears his name.

We have a lot of exploring to do—even more Disney treasure to unpack. We do hope you will learn some things about Disney you never knew before, and more importantly we hope you'll discover some new things about yourself and your life's adventure.

Disney was the threshold for so much wonder, surprise, and delight in my life. But, friends, there's more to discover beyond the castle.

Let's see if our shared journey can become a gateway for the discovery of *your* happily ever after.

I wrote this story for you, but when I began it I had not realized that girls grow quicker than books. As a result you are already too old for fairy tales, and by the time it is printed and bound you will be older still. But some day you will be old enough to start reading fairy tales again.

C. S. Lewis, in the dedication of
The Lion, the Witch, and the Wardrobe
to his goddaughter, Lucy
(New York: Macmillan, 1950)

CHAPTER 1

VACITIONS
Adventure Awaits

Walt Disney said, "It was all started by a mouse." In my case, it was all started by a family vacation to the magical kingdom the mouse built. I will never forget my first trip to Walt Disney World in 1971, just three months after the park opened. The details are still so clear. Crossing into Florida with the smell of oranges blowing through the open windows of our wood-paneled station wagon with its pop-up third seat. Riding the monorail across the Seven Seas Lagoon to arrive at the Magic Kingdom. Standing on Main Street, jaw-dropped in awe at the sight of the Cinderella Castle. Tasting a Citrus Swirl in Adventureland for the first time. And actually *driving* the Grand Prix Raceway cars with my big brother over and over again.

Days before Christmas, we traveled from our home in Columbus, Ohio to Orlando. Now we have to stop here in my story because I need to tell you that I am Christmas crazy. I love this time of year when the world comes alive in anticipation. Our senses are on full alert—lights are brighter, sounds are purer, and fragrances are more alluring. It isn't about the unwrapping for me. In fact, it's all about the wrapping and the sights and sounds that proclaim a clearer message of joy than we hear in our day-to-day routine. For an admitted "Christmas Crazy," Disney decked out for the holidays is sheer magic.

I witnessed firsthand what the pictures could only hint at, especially at night: Cinderella Castle all aglow, carolers lining the streets, and fireworks lighting up the sky in red and green. Some people would say it was over the top. (Maybe over the top and back again.) But for a ten-year-old who had never seen anything like it—*amazing!*

Grandma Ilia, Mom, and the kids take on Disney World.

So back to this Disney World road trip. In the family station wagon were Mom and Dad, my older brother Chip (always my partner in Disney adventures), my little sister Fifi (whose actual name is Jill, but since she is the family pet, so adorable and fun, Fifi fit better), and Baby Mike (the "favorite," our mascot and the quintessential youngest child). The Carbiener family had two sibling groups—the big kids (me and Chip) and the babies (Fifi and Baby Mike). My grandparents, Ilia and Pople, also traveled with us on this visit, which made it all the more memorable. My grandmother Ilia never met a trip or an adventure she didn't want to take. Barely five-feet tall, she would throw back her shoulders, own all sixty inches of her height, and make her way. Pople was a friend to everyone. He collected friends and their stories like treasured souvenirs.

Dad, Mom, and the Big Kids conquer the Magic Kingdom.

We stayed just outside of Walt Disney World in the Dutch Inn, located in Lake Buena Vista (the city The Walt Disney Company named for the Buena Vista Street location of its Burbank, California world headquarters). The hotel was still under construction, and I remember people working nonstop to complete it. The innkeepers openly acknowledged being behind the construction schedule, but because they didn't want to cancel Christmastime reservations, they finished construction with an audience.

Imagine being a child and waking up in Disney World on Christmas morning. Santa and Disney are an irresistible combination for a child. (Who am I kidding? For just about anyone.) We woke up that morning to discover Santa loved Disney World too, and he'd found his way to the Dutch Inn. Chip and I might have been a little too old to truly believe, but for the sake of the babies. . . and just in case. . . .

Each of us received watches from Santa. I was given my first Disney watch: the classic Cinderella watch with a powder-blue strap. We attended a church service crowded with people gathered from who knows where. As we all sang "Joy to the World," it seemed to me that much of the big world was there in that room. That was the first time I realized how many people from so many places can come together for one purpose. During that service we experienced "a small world," making Disney even more exotic to this already wide-eyed ten-year-old.

My mental scrapbook of that first visit includes watching the parades in the afternoon and again at night, riding Pirates of the Caribbean with my dad, who held my hand and let me sit close (without letting on that he knew I was scared), and the entire family singing—practically screaming—to Country Bear Jamboree. (The Jamboree was Baby Mike's favorite. He later worked there for a summer job.) And what visit was complete without enough boat rides through It's a Small World to put us all into a Small World coma? Feeling quite grown-up, we took the babies on Dumbo and then left them with Mom and Dad, making it clear they weren't old enough to drive the race cars like we big kids were. And, oh, the Grand Prix cars. I could spend an entire chapter on Chip and me running back and forth to the cars, each driving our own and feeling so independent, with our official Grand Prix driver's licenses to prove it.

Walt Disney World Take Two

The minute we arrived home from our first trip, we started pestering Mom and Dad to return. Disney World had become our place. But a place that special was a splurge, and we couldn't go every year. That was part of what I learned from those early visits—planning, saving, and anticipating are part of the fun. I couldn't recognize it at the time, but as a child I was living the mantra "It's not just the [Disney] destination, but the journey that counts." Our family would talk and dream about the next trip, enjoying the anticipation. The big kids would earn spending money through odd jobs and squirrel away any gift money we'd receive. And we'd plot our route and itinerary with maps and guidebooks all around.

Based largely on these early vacations and the planning for them, I fell in love with the "before," finding that "afters" are more satisfying when you've paid attention to the before. I came to appreciate that in the planning of an adventure I could enjoy a vacation even before I left home. Three years after our first Disney vacation we had saved, imagined, and planned enough to return. This time we were even going to stay right next door to the Magic Kingdom in the Polynesian Village Resort.

From the start, that second trip was a different and greater adventure. We refer to it as the Disney "cow" trip. Mom and Dad were always trying to enrich us with new experiences. Mom was the schemer and dreamer and, true to form, Dad was the master planner and logistics officer. This time they decided we needed to take a train to Disney World. Train travel was becoming less frequent, and my parents wanted us to know what it was like to "ride the rails." They booked our travel on the Auto-Train, a privately owned railroad that provided service from Louisville, Kentucky and other Mid-Atlantic cities to central Florida.

The Auto-Train allowed passengers and their automobiles to travel to Florida together for $450 for one car and two passengers. Automobiles were loaded into double-deck carrier cars while passengers were greeted by young, uniformed hosts directing travelers into dome, dining, or sleeper cars. Think of it; traveling without the hassle of driving but having your car available when you arrived in Florida. Genius! The trip took about twenty-two hours, and the service included meals, live entertainment, movies, and even bingo. It was a fun, forward-thinking service like a cruise ship on rails. (Unfortunately, the company's dreams were bigger than its wallet, and the original Auto-Train went bankrupt ten years later.)

Well, I like to think our Auto-Train experience was even more exciting than most, thanks to Bessie. On our first trip to the buffet car the train encountered a cow playing chicken on the tracks. The emergency brakes screeched, stutter-stopping us to a halt and sending everyone and everything flying. Big Brother Chip ended up with his tray of food over his chest, mashed potatoes dotted with green peas coating his shirt. Dad landed on his behind on the floor, babies safely on top of him. And then there was Grandma Ilia. The sudden stop launched her into the wide-mouthed trash bin. Headfirst. All we could see of her were her little legs flapping in the air.

Once Mom and I realized that everyone was okay, we got the giggles. And I don't mean contained, polite giggles. I mean the laugh-so-hard-you-can't-stop giggles. The my-side-hurts and I-just-snorted giggles. My dad thought he'd scowl us into silence, but that made us laugh harder. Eventually we pulled Grandma from the trash bin and wiped Chip clean. No one was hurt—well, except for the reckless cow. And this encounter taught me at a young age that when the flow doesn't go, make the best of it. Even an abrupt stop can add to the adventure.

Cow stop notwithstanding, we made it to Walt Disney World and once again the trip was a *blast*. The Polynesian Village remains my favorite Disney resort because I so vividly remember walking into the entrance atrium, entranced by its exotic trees and birds. We were greeted with "Alohas" and served island-inspired punch and cookies. Our room was themed to tropical perfection. Truly, we'd found paradise.

To Save and Savor

I mentioned that we had learned to save for our second trip to Disney World. I have always liked to work, and I earmarked my early earnings for Disney trips and the souvenirs and gifts I would take home. If I received a little money for my birthday, I would add that to my stash, which I kept secure in an envelope covered in Disney stickers. I would count (and recount) my cash, imagining the collection of souvenirs I might bring home. My favorite Disney purchases were my first stuffed Mickey, the mouse ears with my name embroidered on them, and a light blue T-shirt with Mickey on it. I could show you them all—but I wouldn't attempt trying on the shirt. Though classics never go out of style, they do seem to get smaller with time.

We made a few more family trips to Disney World before Chip and I, the big kids, left for college. After we left, the babies and Mom and Dad continued to visit. And anytime the six of us could be together at Disney World, we jumped at the chance. One Christmas we all found temporary employment as cast members. (Well, all of us except Dad. He said he already had a job.)

I can't overstate the significance of those vacations and how they set the stage for what was to come. So much to unpack. So many souvenirs that I carry with me today. I learned to read maps by Dad explaining the Disney World guidebooks on that first trip, a precursor to my job as a Disney tour guide. When our trip planning led us to a dead end, I learned to abandon the plan. And there I discovered that sometimes a plan gone bad is best. I have realized that spending time with people we love is a gift that we have to schedule into our lives. Like nothing else can, vacations provide us with treasure, trash, and trail mix: the things we keep, the things we toss, and the things we sort through the rest of our lives.

Disney World and a Paycheck Too?

And then there was my "vacation of destiny."

Since I seemed to spend most of my savings on Disney vacations, what could be better than working at Disney for a summer job? (Not that I would lose focus and leave college without a diploma, Dad. Don't worry. It's just a summer job.) I was a freshman at the University of Kentucky when a group of us headed to Florida for spring break to stay with the grandmother of our friend Nancy (Scott), my best pal in adventure. We cooked up a stop at Disney on the way. Being fearless and a little clueless we drove right to the Casting Center and said, "We're here for a summer job. We want to work at Disney."

Amazingly enough we were taken seriously and admitted to the Casting Center where we were required to take a math test with questions like "If Donald has $30.00 and he spends $12.75, how much is left?" Disney character references throughout an employment test, of all things!

Janis (Petrie), the queen of casting, hired me. Janis was a Disney poster child with her infectious smile and warm personality. Believe me, to meet her is to be her friend. And so began our cherished friendship. Right from the start, Janis embodied the slogan "Join the company, join the family." At one point, those worlds converged, when Janis hired everyone in my family to work at Disney (except Dad, who *continued* to remind us he already had a job).

While my group of friends and I were applying for Disney summer jobs, we learned about a prototype program called the Magic Kingdom College Program. When we asked about participating, we were told the University of Kentucky wasn't part of the initial rollout. Well, Nance and I couldn't stand for that, so promptly upon our return to campus we met with our internship coordinators. Months later, we packed our suitcases and headed to Walt Disney World for the inaugural summer season of Disney's college program.

The Magic Kingdom College Program, now called The Walt Disney World College Program, was such a blast. What could be better than working at Disney, living with a group of college kids from around the country (and today, with Epcot, students from around the world), and learning about the company—all the while earning college credits? *Yay!* Dad was always skeptical about that last bit. A baccalaureate earned with credits in fairy tales, fries, and boat rides? Doubtful. But lo and behold, the credits materialized. And, truly, we did attend classes several times a week on serious subjects like finance, service, and operations.

The best part? We lived in Snow White Village, a nearby Kissimmee campground, populated with double-wide trailers specifically designated for summer interns. The accommodations may have been slightly substandard, but we loved them. Our double-wide came complete with a tiny bedroom, mini-kitchen with a foldout table, and a sitting room. The daily offering from that tiny kitchen was some combination of Jell-O, macaroni and cheese, and tuna straight from the can.

Since at that time the attractions in the Magic Kingdom were open until midnight and Main Street until 1:00 a.m. (to encourage last-minute souvenir shopping), most of the college kids worked the night shift from 6:00 p.m. to 2:00 a.m. That meant our days were spent at the beach (about an hour's drive) or by the pool. Our accommodations were no Polynesian Village, but we did manage to get a Polynesian tan. Who knew then that the primary offering of the Sunshine State could exact a toll on its fair-skinned visitors?

That first summer went by fast. I was having so much fun that my dad worried I might stay. Though tempted, Nancy was a nursing student and had to return to her coursework. Reluctantly, I went with her.

But I returned the next summer—the park's tenth anniversary. "The Happiest Happy Birthday ever!" I auditioned for the Tencennial Parade and got a job as a "summer swing." I learned all the routines for every female character on parade so that I could fill in for full-time parade performers who were on vacation. My friends Cyd (Cunningham) and Sue (Trembly) were hired to work in Operations in Tomorrowland, both of them sporting mod polyester jumpsuits. Our friend Sara Gray (Horne) landed perhaps the best assignment of all—a job in the Main Street Confectionary. We visited her often on our days off. You know, to encourage her, and taste-test the goodies.

Howdy, partner! I always had a blast dancing the hoedown with Alex in the Magic Kingdom parade.

Entertainment is really the heartbeat of Disney, and I will always be grateful for the opportunity to have danced in the parades. From the Frontierland hoedown two-step to the parade version of the Diamond Horseshoe Saloon can-can, I learned to smile (always), to keep dancing even when I don't feel it, and to pay attention to the audience, whose enthusiasm can energize you. Because despite working in my dream job, some days dancing the can-can seemed like work. More like, I can't-can't. It's hot-hot. Please, not again. Then the music would start, I'd lock eyes with a clapping guest, and pure pixie dust! I would again realize that I was making Disney magic. In those moments, I learned how to enjoy a parade from the inside out.

When my dad suggested I might not be able to can-can my way through a career, I left my pantaloons and light-up ball gown and the happiest happy birthday ever to return to campus. (Sigh.) But a short nineteen months later, I graduated with a bachelor's degree and accepted my first professional job—a position in Walt Disney World Guest Relations. You could say I ended up where our first vacation started.

From that first position, I moved in and around the company, holding some twenty-two different positions from parade dancer to senior vice president in the Office of the Chairman. What a journey. Denny (Rydberg), Young Life's retired president, has said: "When God wants to teach you something, He takes you on a trip." And so it has been with me.

The Magic of Vacation

Vacations call us away from home and out of our comfort zones too. We eat new foods, explore new places, and go deeper in our thinking. Most often, we move out of the familiar with someone we love by our side. Nothing connects you to someone else like shared discovery and adventure. I think it's what we were created for. Maybe that's why family vacations and Disney theme parks captured my heart from an early age and never let go.

The same may be true for you. Your first trip to a Disney theme park may have been to Disney World, like me. Or maybe you visited Disneyland. Cast members there proudly identify it as "the original." Wherever you first encountered a Disney theme park, with thousands of others who were also there that day, somehow that experience was yours alone. My friend and colleague, Jeff Kurtti, author of *Disneyland—From Once upon a Time to Happily Ever After*, has written about this phenomenon: "The bricks and mortar of the place itself may remain exactly as they have been for decades, but the encounter of each individual visitor, their own emotional reactions, and their own method in passing along that occurrence creates a place at once shared by millions, and as personal as a first kiss."[1]

Disney experiences feature prominently in the childhood memories of so many, and yet the Disney brothers themselves had a childhood that was hardly "Disney" idyllic. They resolved to provide for others the opportunities they lacked. Walt envisioned vacation destinations that were neat, clean, and fun. Places that could be enjoyed by family members of all ages. Sure, they made money doing it, but I will never believe that was the primary driver.

Instead, I think the words on the Walt Disney World dedication plaque at the base of the Main Street flagpole capture the heart of it. Thousands pass by the plaque every day without giving it a first or a second glance. On October 25, 1971, Roy O. Disney, Walt's brother, read its message at the grand opening of the park:

Walt Disney World is a tribute to the philosophy and life of Walter Elias Disney and to the talents, the dedication, and the loyalty of the entire Disney organization that made Walt Disney's dream come true. May Walt Disney World bring Joy and Inspiration and New Knowledge to all who come to this happy place . . . a Magic Kingdom where the young at heart of all ages can laugh and play and learn . . . together.

Two months later, days before my family and I visited Disney World for the first time, Roy died. His words, memorialized in bronze, were true for my family in 1971 and still ring true for me today. And now, let's walk through the castle doors and beyond to bring some Disney magic into our day-to-day lives.

SCENTS AND SENSIBILITIES

The human nose detects between four thousand and ten thousand unique scents. And when we think we are tasting something, we may actually be smelling it. (Eat a jellybean while pinching your nose. Can you tell its flavor?) We smell flavor.

Disney imagineers know that. They also know that unlike our other senses, smell is hardwired to our brain (not dissembled or remixed), and it travels a short path to the area of the brain that handles emotions. That's why smell can transport us to a time and feeling that we'd long forgotten.

Think of your favorite Disney smells. Maybe it's the familiar and still enticing smell of Main Street popcorn, or the musty leather and gunpowder smell that wafts out of the Pirates of the Caribbean ride. Those scents are emitted courtesy of a Disney-patented technology called the Scent-Emitting Systems, or as we knew it, the "Smellitzer." If you've taken a ride on Soarin' at Disney California Adventure, you know firsthand how the Smellitzer can lead guests by the nose. Whether the citrusy smell of the orange groves, the salty smell of the Pacific Ocean, or the pine scent along the ski hills, these aromas transport you in a way that a visual or auditory experience alone cannot.

Walt himself said, "Always, as you travel assimilate the sights and sounds of the world."[2] And my first visits to Disney World taught me that magical memories are sensory dimensional. In my future assignments, I would use "common sense" to check for the engagement of smell, sight, sound, taste, and touch, with the hope that we would delight guests across the spectrum of senses and that they would remember their Disney theme park visits with the same warm feelings I do even today.

CHAPTER 2

TIARAS
Know Thyself

Maybe you work with some princesses. (We all know the type.) But when I say I worked with princesses, I really, truly worked with princesses—of the fictional variety, anyway. And one year we had a princess problem of kingdom magnitude.

Folks in Disney Consumer Products were orchestrating princess paloozas, assembling great casts of princesses and having them appear together on Disney merchandise—from T-shirts to toys, backpacks to travel mugs, and almost any other trinket you could imagine. Up to this point, the princesses hadn't traveled far from their neighborhoods, only appearing with the other characters in their respective animated worlds. For example, Snow White might sing and dance with the dwarfs in the woods, but you wouldn't see her swimming with Ariel under the sea. And Mulan wouldn't drop into a nineteenth-century French village, nor would Pocahontas paddle up the fjords of Arendelle. It just wasn't done.

And then there was the related issue of Tinker Bell. Did Tinker Bell have a legitimate claim to the throne? Was she a princess just because she was a girl, or was she something else altogether?

So What's a Princess, Anyway?

Enter Roy E. Disney, the company's vice chairman, nephew of Walt, and son of Roy O. Disney, who had seen some of this merchandise and considered it confusing and not "in character" (a Disney term) with the princesses pictured. I was given the charge to respond to Roy's concern because I was leading Disney Corporate Synergy at the time. Our department's primary responsibility was ensuring that all of our divisions collaborated for the greater good, and the princess palooza problem became ours to untangle. The issue was roundly discussed inside and outside of Disney. Extracting the female characters from their films and assembling them as a distinct "Disney Princess Brand" was a topic of interest to merchandisers and media alike, including the UK's *The Economist*, which reported, "Disney's definition of a princess is elastic. A mermaid, Ariel, is included, and there was a weighty strategic debate over whether also to count Tinkerbell (sic), a fairy."[1]

One meeting among many stands out to me, one convened to answer the all-important—if not eternal—question, "What's a princess?" Cast members gathered from every division of the company: Theme Parks, Studios, Animation, Television, and Consumer Products. There were attendees from our marketing and product development departments, along with designers, artists, and writers. Anyone who had a vested interest in the future of the "Disney Princess" was invited to the meeting I called the "Princess Summit." Which was pretty much the entire company. If you worked at Disney, you were passionate about princesses.

Emotions ran high. After all, at Disney, the princesses not only made for good (and big) business, they were and are cherished.

This reveals a truth about Disney issues. On the one hand, and in the greater scheme of life, princesses aren't a big deal. Right? But in the daily operations of Disney, every seemingly insignificant decision—even (or especially) about princesses—could have far-reaching consequences. A little misstep could become *big* news. And a small mistake could tarnish the legendary Disney sparkle.

Nieces Jen, Jess, and Meg with "Cindy" in her royal banquet hall all decked out for Christmas.

Still, even in the midst of our princess project, I had to smile. Some people spend their days discussing cash flow, staffing, workplace safety, and other critical business issues, but there we were, discussing the makeup of a princess. And was Tinker Bell in or out? But these are the types of Disney decisions that left to interpretation can turn kingdom magic into kingdom mayhem.

I'll dispense with the details, but suffice it to say, there was much loud discussion, disagreement, and gnashing of teeth. (In a polite, princess-worthy sort of way.) In the end, Disney established the required criteria for an entry-level princess. These criteria are still being nuanced today, as they will be tomorrow, in a continuing process of refinement, which is a key point worth noting: in business and in life, the essential issues deserve regular discussion.

You Might Be a Princess If . . .

Out of these discussions emerged the six essentials of a Disney Princess:

✳ **Number One: A princess must be a royal**—either by birth or by marriage. Pocahontas, for example, is the daughter of the chief. She's in. Ariel, daughter of Triton, ruler of Atlantica, is a natural. Belle, on the other hand, falls for a Beast (problem!) who of course turns out to be a prince (such a kidder), and she marries him. Belle's a keeper.

Some might argue that Mulan fails the princess litmus test on this first criterion, but remember, she saves her native land. None other than the emperor himself honors Mulan for her courage and service to China. That seems more than adequate. Mulan's in.

And what about Tinker Bell? Against this measure, Tinker Bell certainly is not a princess. (Sorry, Tink.)

Number Two: A princess must have some royal rags. This was important for the proper princess look that comes into play, especially in merchandise. Now, rest assured, a princess doesn't always wear her ball gown. (Mulan is the best example of this.) Furthermore, she might not own or wear a ball gown until later in her life. Consider Cinderella, forced to wear rags and scrub floors by her evil stepmother until she was transformed by her fairy godmother. Part of that "bibbidi-bobbidi" transformation included a beautiful ball gown. Here again, Tinker Bell fails the princess test. Tunic and slippers? (Hmm, sorry, Tink. But your wings are awesome.)

Aurora has some stories to share
and dreams to deliver to niece Jen.

✳ **Number Three: A princess must have loyal pals.** Whether a furry friend (or two) or a comical sidekick, a princess's faithful friends cause the sun to shine a little brighter.

✳ **Number Four: A princess must have a transformational experience.** Every princess in the ensemble has an "aha moment" when she becomes who she was always meant to be. Each one meets her destiny. Sleeping Beauty, finger-pricked into a deep sleep according to the curse of the evil Maleficent, awakens to her calling through true love's kiss and becomes the princess of her destiny. Belle, the bookish inventor's daughter, transforms alongside the Beast to become a princess. Mulan, fearless and bold, assumes the appearance of a boy to lead the fight for her family's honor, and in doing so discovers her inner strength. And Tinker Bell? Once a pixie, always a pixie. (Oh, Tink.)

✳ **Number Five: A princess must have redeeming qualities of kindness, caring, sincerity, and hope.** She never wavers, even if these qualities sometimes get her into trouble. Remember when Snow White pities the Evil Queen disguised as an old beggar woman and eats the poisonous apple? Her innate kindness is her undoing. This doesn't mean that our Disney Princess can't be brave or feisty like Mulan or Merida, or bullheaded like Ariel when she runs away from home. But at their core, kindness, courage, caring, conviction, and hope always win out. Princesses exercise those virtues to make their world a better place.

And last but not least . . .

✱ **Number Six: Bring on Prince Charming!** What would a princess be without her ever-loving, ever-faithful knight in shining armor? Snow White sings, "Someday my prince will come," and at Disney, he always does. (Castle side note: This was before *Frozen*, which introduced "evil" princes and heroes that come in the form of little sisters, or even in the form of voyagers like Moana, who stand on their own without a love interest or ball gown. These modern heroines still experience transformation, but it's more like self-discovery. A *Time Magazine* writer said of Moana's transformative journey that it's as if she is asking, "What's wrong with me?" And haven't we all asked the same question? The writer goes on to say, "The answer is no less poignant for our having guessed it—that is, absolutely nothing."[2] But I digress.)

Out of that season of heated debate came a plan and, eventually, the guidelines that would help our cast members make good decisions about proper princess placement. Lilo, Alice in Wonderland, and Tinker Bell would not appear on merchandise with the princesses. But don't be sad for them. They're doing quite well for themselves.

We also set new parameters on how the princesses could interact with each other while staying true to their worlds. At any time, you might see a panoply of princesses, but they won't be under the sea at Ariel's place. We developed generic princess playgrounds that don't jeopardize the integrity of their individual characters. And wherever a Disney aficionado discovers a discrepancy, you can bet the exception is no accident, but a robustly discussed decision.

Sounds life-altering, yes? Let me tell you, I got a chuckle telling the story of the initial meeting to my dad, the nuclear engineer with a doctoral degree. Enjoying the contrast between our life's work, I called to update him: "Dad, I know how proud you are that I am making such a difference in the world doing really important work. So here is what I did today: I convened a Princess Summit." (No, it wasn't atomic, but I think he might have been just a little envious.)

So the decision wasn't rocket science, or brain surgery either, but it might have been brand surgery, and no small matter. With the Princess Summit, Disney had averted a potential crisis. By establishing what constitutes a princess, into the future and as the characters age, the princesses will remain true to themselves. If any princess has a film with a sequel, the artists, directors, and producers will continue her story and build on its rich history, entertaining us for years to come. And the ancillary products that personalize her will stay on point and enhance the storylines.

So outside of Disney, how does a princess summit apply to life? In so many ways. Let's explore the three principles that, when applied to the business of commerce or life, can themselves be transformational. In proper princess vernacular:

Know thyself.

Know thy purpose.

To thine own self be true.

Know Thyself (So You're Not a Princess)

Not everyone can be a princess, and that's okay. (Really, it is.) We may aspire to royalty and want all the advantages that come with the title, but for many of us, it just isn't in our blood. It's not our destiny, our calling, or our rightful place.

And while you might nod your head to that obvious statement, do you still find yourself looking at someone else's perfect life and wishing you could trade places? Do you yearn for someone else's talents? Do you dream of dancing in a ballroom in a fancy gown and bemoan the fact that all you can do is fly?

It bears repeating: Tinker Bell, Alice in Wonderland, and Lilo—all without a spot on the Disney Princess roster—are still having a big ol' time.

Take Tinker Bell. *Not a princess*. But here is the great news: She *is* a pixie. She has a fun, impish personality and—quite possibly the best in my book—she hangs out all day in Neverland. (You know, the place where dreams are born and time is never planned.)

But even better: Tinker Bell *flies!*

It's not only okay to be Tinker Bell, it's *great* to be Tinker Bell! Don't waste any time crying over a castle you may never call home.

Go. *Fly. Soar!* Take off to the places only you can reach, like the spires of Cinderella Castle. Go set off some fireworks!

Each of us needs to find our true selves, the person God created us to be. Uniquely you. Uniquely me. But how do you know if you have wings to fly, or the head for a crown? Resources abound to help you in the discovery. It's been nearly two decades since the Gallup organization introduced an online tool to help people identify five dominant talent themes, which together with your skills and knowledge make up your differentiating strengths and what they call a "signature theme."[3] The assessment isolates thirty-four different talents (inborn predispositions) that set in the right environment and enhanced with experience and training, will allow you to fly—or govern your kingdom—with ease and near-perfect precision.

What interests me about the Gallup premise is this: Instead of calling out your weaknesses and expending energy to minimize or eliminate them (and getting depressed over the sum total of them), you lean into your strengths and let them propel you. This school of thought doesn't deny the blind spots or scarcity of some talents you many have. Instead, it invites you to attend your own personal princess summit: Are you a princess or not? There's no shame in lacking a talent for ideation and competition if you recognize your predisposition to empathy and strategy. The key is to rightly assess who you are, what you offer, and what you lack, and then to quickly learn the corollary—people around you are gifted with talents you do not naturally possess. Affirm those strangers who are so unlike you (the very ones who drive you crazy from time to time) and realize that your contributions to the world will amount to less without them. In fact, your own life experience will be diminished without the gifts only they can offer.

What if these tools had existed back in the day, when Mickey was not yet a cash cow and the name Disney had not become the standard-bearer of excellence in family entertainment? I'm guessing Walt would have been flush in ideation, future-thinking, and optimism. Surely characteristics like these drove him through the early development years of Snow White when the film (which later earned enough money to build Disney's Burbank Campus) was ridiculed as "Disney's Folly." Enter older brother Roy, likely more analytical, consistent, and deliberative. He was more of a realist. But when Disney Studios ran out of the cash to continue paying Snow White's 750 animators and artists, who came up with the plan to show the in-process movie to the bank executive whose loan would bring Snow White to life? Walt had older brother Roy-the-realist to thank for that.

And speaking of the analytical Roy O., it's worth noting that if you abide by the assessment tool's assertion that there are thirty-four distinct strengths, the chance that you would meet someone with your top five strengths is about 1 in 278,000. The likelihood of meeting someone with the same rank order of those top five talents? That's a slim 1 in 33 million.

We need to know ourselves and remain true to who we are. While we never stop making the best of our strengths and experiences, or acknowledging and seeking reinforcements for our weaknesses, we needn't spend precious time wanting to be something we are not.

When you recognize your unique makeup and value the personalities of the people in your life, you grab hold of the opportunity to become the expert at your life's work—whether that's in a boardroom or on a construction site—or in a family room that just happens to look like a construction site.

This lifelong quest can be an exhilarating adventure. The joy is found in the journey, in the daily discovery of our calling as we work alongside others who are discovering theirs. And princess or fairy, we can all practice scattering a little appreciation over those we journey with. Because the wonderful thing about being Tinker Bell is that a sprinkling of her pixie dust allows others to fly too.

Walt's Folly

When rumored cost overruns and production delays in the making of *Snow White* led skeptics to call the film "Disney's Folly," according to Walt's daughter, Diane, one trusted adviser told him to let the rumors fly. Al Horne said, "Your best policy is to keep everybody wondering. If they keep wondering, they'll keep talking. In that way you'll have free promotion based on sheer curiosity."[8]

You'd have thought the millions *Snow White* earned following its 1938 release would have silenced Walt's critics or that Disney would never again be threatened by failure. Well, yes and no. He would teeter on the edge of failure again. And again.

Disneyland opened on July 17, 1955, weeks before it was ready to welcome guests. Some attractions were unfinished and hidden behind buntings. Restaurants ran out of food. A plumbers' strike made bathrooms scarce necessities. The expected attendance of five thousand guests tallied closer to twenty-eight thousand because of counterfeit tickets. And this opening day fiasco was captured in ninety minutes of live television. An unsympathetic Hollywood press called Disneyland "Walt's Nightmare."

But those critics didn't dissuade folks from visiting. Within two months, Disneyland had welcomed its one millionth guest. By July 1956, attendance topped three and a half million. Heartened, Disney went on to develop another theme park in a swampland in central Florida. What a crazy idea. Doomed. Except . . . it wasn't.

Disney had no fear of failure (though maybe he should have had some healthy respect for it). He said, "It's important to have a good hard failure when you're young. I learned a lot out of that. Because it makes you kind of aware of what can happen to you. Because of it I've never had any fear in my whole life when we've been near collapse and all of that. I've never been afraid. I've never had the feeling I couldn't walk out and get a job doing something."[9]

What's come of Disney's Nightmare? At its sixty-year anniversary in 2015, Disneyland had surpassed total overall attendance of 750 million guests. That's a nightmare Disney only dreamed about.

Know Thy Purpose
(Or, It's Okay to Be Tinker Bell)

Purpose unlocks passion, and passion produces.

Organizations, including businesses, churches, teams, and families, thrive when groups of talented people, well trained and striving for excellence, come together and make magic. But it isn't magic. It's work. And that work is intentional. The magic is the product of every team member knowing their role, bringing their talents to work every day, and offering their very best. The magic happens when we uncover our true vocation and then go after it.

The writer and theologian Frederick Buechner said of our

true vocation, "By and large a good rule for finding out is this: the kind of work God usually calls you to is the kind of work (a) that you need most to do and (b) that the world most needs to have done. . . . The place God calls you to is the place where your deep gladness and the world's deep hunger meet."[4]

The Disney mission can be (and once was) summed up in four little words: To make people happy. Does the world long for happiness? Yes. Now more than ever. And do Disney cast members discover deep gladness trying to make the world a happier place? This cast member did.

Knowing your purpose applies not only to you personally, but also to your organization or sphere of influence. Mary (Tomlinson), a dear friend of mine with a consulting practice called On Purpose Partners, consults with and trains both individuals and companies to help them stay true to their core. She says this: "Purpose answers the 'why' and aligns personal and organizational behavior." She says, "We lose our *way* because we've lost our *why*."[5]

More often than not, when individuals and organizations falter, it's because they've lost sight of who they are and what they are uniquely designed to do. It doesn't mean that you can't grow and expand, but remember, success is knowing your "why" and your "what," and doing that well. Simply put, you can't be all things to all people. You must focus, train, and be the best at being you.

What's your purpose? Why do you get out of bed each and every day? What positions you to be successful? Are there areas where you are struggling and others where you, like Tinker Bell, are soaring? Maybe it's time to reconsider those places where you have extended yourself out of your core competencies, and possibly out of your center of joy. Conversely, growth could be just what you need, but perhaps not so quickly.

The Curious Thing about Passion

Maybe your current situation calls you to wait tables, crunch numbers, or manage through the diaper days. If you don't feel particularly passionate about your work or your life, what then? Quite simply, it's this: Commit to serve, crunch, and manage well.

Often, we don't follow our passion. It follows *us* when we apply ourselves to the work at hand. And in that work—inconsequential as it may seem at the time—we may discover a talent or gift that fuels our passion. You may find you are a team leader, encourager, organizer, or entrepreneur cleverly disguised as a housekeeper.

Or what if you'd love to be passionate, but you just don't know what to be passionate about? What if you have more than one passion—and even more that you're curious about?

That curiosity may lead you to passion's door. Walt Disney said, "We keep moving forward—opening new doors and doing new things—because we're curious. And curiosity keeps leading us down new paths."[6]

When you can't be passionate about your life, be curious. Take the risk of allowing your curiosity to lead you. As Mary and Bert sing in the stage production of *Mary Poppins*, "Open different doors, you may find a you there that you never knew was yours."[7]

Consider this Disney example. Club Disney was a concept that seemed to be a natural extension for Disney: regionally based learning and play centers geared toward young kids. Parents were encouraged to bring their children for a fun time out, a party, or a little Disney adventure. Turns out we weren't prepared to be in the drop-off child day care business, and we never intended that to be the experience. Parents expected the clubs to be mini Disney theme parks in their own backyard. When Cinderella Castle, the boats from It's a Small World, and a crew of characters didn't materialize inside the doors, we had already disappointed our target audience. And for the parents expecting Mary Poppins to supervise their children, even a spoonful of sugar wasn't going to appease.

Two years after opening, the play centers closed. It was a fitting and seemingly natural extension for Disney that didn't succeed. But Disney fell forward—and with style. Employees at the facilities were offered other jobs within Disney, the computers and learning tools in the centers were donated to area schools, and unsold merchandise in the clubs was donated to the local Toys for Tots holiday drive. If you're going to fall—and we all will—fall forward. Let every struggle help you discover something more about your purpose, and every failure move you closer to living your passion.

To Thine Own Self Be True
(Or, Work It, Tinker Bell!)

Once you know yourself and your purpose, be true to *your* story. The Princess Summit was really a corporate pronouncement of the truth that all integrity is lost if characters are not living out their stories, and only their stories. Likewise, our stories have authentic characters, settings, and plotlines that can't be interchanged, borrowed, or over-manipulated. And though we can hang out with characters from other kingdoms, we shouldn't forget where we come from or who we are.

Jasmine lives in Agrabah and can fly on the magic carpet with Aladdin. What would happen if the Disney animators wrote a sequel and the opening scene featured Ariel joining her on the magic carpet and, with the Genie, they buzz Belle's castle? Even the greatest storyteller would have trouble making that connection. What we learned at Disney is that story disconnects cause confusion and out-of-context characters will eventually suffer identity crises. Your story is yours, your kingdom is yours, and your magic is yours. And that's the way it should be.

Your Personal Princess Summit

Maybe you're wondering what would happen if you were to convene a personal princess summit. Day to day, what would be the difference? The difference is, everything changes. Never again will you waver over the truth of who you are and what you were created to do. In that truth lies your success; not acclaim or financial reward, though possibly that too, but a deeper satisfaction, a sense of purpose, living the life you were called to, and knowing your life has meaning.

Now hear this: Bad days will come. Prevailing conditions will ground you, and you won't soar. You won't even get a lift. But even if your wings are temporarily clipped, you will remember you were meant to fly. And soon enough, you will. (Unless you're a princess—in which case, refer to guidelines #2 and #6. You have a ball gown and a prince. Go dance, princess. Go dance!)

PRINCESS—OR PIXIE

Snow White is the youngest Disney Princess, perennially fourteen. (Far too young to care for so many dwarfs, in my opinion.) And she is also the heroine in Disney's first-ever fully animated, feature-length film. When the attraction Snow White's Scary Adventures opened at Disneyland in 1955, Snow White was missing in action. Riders were intended to experience the ride as her. In 1994 the ride was renovated, and for the first time, Snow White had a place in her own theme park adventure.

She may have missed a few years at her own adventure, but she's the only princess to have a star on the Hollywood Walk of Fame. You know who else has a star? Tinker Bell. I'm telling you: it's okay to be Tink.

It's good to be Tinker Bell.
(And niece Jess knows it.)

CHAPTER 3

WHAT'S INSIDE
Cultivating Integrity

A*nimate*: to bring to life. An apt definition because animation—*Disney* animation that is, brought the company to life. That mouse who started it all came to life first on screen, later in television, and then in physical, near-human form in Disneyland. Walt, his brother Roy, and the early animators are truly the founders of the company they brought to life. They gave it shape, personality, and voice. Disney animators and artists carry on that tradition today. (And you will see a nod to that shared heritage in nearly every Pixar film. Look for A113 in your favorites from *Toy Story* to *Inside Out*. The number refers to the California Institute of the Arts classroom where many Disney and Pixar animators were schooled in their craft. The reference is a hidden homage to the alma mater they revere.)[1]

One of those Cal Arts graduates from A113, and one of the most gifted, endearing animators I've had the pleasure of working with is Glen (Keane). Glen is the creator of Ariel, Tarzan, Aladdin, Rapunzel, the Beast, and other characters you know and love. As a thoughtful man, deeply committed to what's inside, he could

51

get to the very soul of his characters. His depiction of the Beast demonstrated his insightfulness. I have often reflected on the broader application of a truth Glen shared that helped him create the Beast—the prince was always there within the Beast.

Some of my fabulous fun fam (the babies) charming the Beast.

Glen approaches most of his animations believing that he gives shape to characters that preexist. "I've always had this feeling that on any character I've animated, that the character existed before I started to draw it, and it was—it's a little bit like Michelangelo sculpting in stone and freeing the figure that's within."[2] Identifying and then freeing the form within is a mighty endeavor. But it's also something individuals and organizations talk about and practice all the time when we talk about brands and branding.

As old as the Greek word *logos*—which means, among other things, "reason" and "expression"—is our interest in identifying the essence of a person or an organization, or the authentic core.

Crystallizing and communicating that essence is an art and strategic business pursuit we know as branding. Efforts to refresh or reinvent the brand command attention and *lots* of money. Yet often, folks on a brand mission ask the wrong questions, less committed to freeing what's within and more interested in reshaping and sometimes contorting their identity to hitch a ride on a popular trend.

I remember when The Walt Disney Company came under fire for diluting the brand. *Harvard Business Review* summarized the time this way: "All products and services that used the Disney name or characters had an impact on Disney's brand equity. And because of the characters' broad exposure in the marketplace, many consumers had begun to feel that Disney was exploiting its name."[3] Everyone was concerned and reacting to some research that resulted in this alert: Disney was experiencing "brand erosion." I took that to mean people weren't buying what we were selling as much as they once did. If you sense just a little skepticism in that comment, you aren't mistaken. I have no issue with pausing to evaluate, ask questions, and gather information to improve decision making. But, let's be clear. Bias, sampling errors, and misleading questions can taint results. And if jobs are on the line, you'd better make sure the research results are only one of the contributors to your decision making. In this particular discussion, I suspected opinions had been formed beforehand.

With that disclaimer, I will jump to the (not so) groundbreaking conclusion. We determined the company needed more focus on the state of "the brand"—*Pronto*!—and the Corporate Brand Management department was given the mandate. (Inside the company, this department was known a little less affectionately as the "Mickey Cops" or "Brand Police.")

No doubt, the attention was merited. With our theme parks,

characters, movies, and hosts of licensed products, logo use and trademarking of branded products required aggressive management. (Not unlike creating corporate policy to distinguish princesses from pixies.) Most interpretations of the Disney brand stayed within our guidelines, but every now and again an interpretation crossed the line. Occasionally, one vaulted right over it. One of those landed at the feet of Walt's nephew, Roy E. Disney, then board vice chairman. While visiting Tokyo Disneyland, he encountered a colorful cast of characters in a merchandise shop, including lime-green Mickey Mouse plush toys, fire-engine-red Minnies, and fluorescent-pink Plutos. They were ears-to-tail green, red, and pink. He even found some patchwork-quilted plush.

Roy gathered a few of these, and when he returned to his Burbank, California, office, he sent them over to Consumer Products. Roy had summarized it this way: "These don't work." Typical of Roy, he got right to the point and then explained that although the characters can wear costumes, at their core they must stay the same. Mickey and Minnie Mouse have black ears and black tails. While Mickey can don a top hat or a sorcerer's robe, and while Minnie might wear a fur-trimmed dress and carry a muff, neither has a lime-green complexion. Never has. Never will. Costumes may change, but "character" doesn't.

Roy was right to be protective of our characters. They are the cornerstone of the Disney brand. Roy once said, "The thing that distinguishes us from everybody else, and always has and always will, is our past. The goal is to look over our shoulder and see Snow White and Pinocchio and Dumbo standing there saying, 'Be this good.' We shouldn't be intimidated by them—they're an arrow pointing someplace."[4] You see, the real struggle at that time wasn't about logos, slogans, or colorful plush. It was about the heart of the organization.

Eau de Pooh

From my first job in merchandise on Main Street, I thought the cast members in charge of the buying, assortment, and placement of merchandise had the coolest jobs. It became a hobby during my career to find interesting, unique Disney items from places around the world. My friends joined me in my quest. Together we were always on the lookout for unique merch. Over time my collection grew. And grew. Okay, it mushroomed. This explains the fifty bins (*slightly* more) of Disney stuff my husband and I moved across the country to our new home. Such treasure. Today that treasure has been contained to our home's Disney-safe zones—and forbidden in Disney-free zones designated by my husband. (I'll tell you more about him later.)

Let's be honest, though. When I say *treasure*, I use the term loosely. My collection includes a one-of-a-kind Italian leather purse. Too nice to use, it was a gift from my husband, who despite his occasional grumps, acquired it for me in partnership with Virgie, my Disneyana collector accomplice. At the other extreme is another treasure—my Mickey earwax cleaner from Tokyo Disneyland.

Tokyo Disney Resort has always had the zaniest merchandise. And I mean that as a compliment. It's the only park operating as a pure licensee, not 100-percent-owned by The Walt Disney Company. While you might think that ownership relationship could lead it astray, I found the opposite to be true. As solemn stewards of a brand they cherish, management there is always concerned with honoring Walt's vision. That, coupled with their willingness to experiment with public-pleasing merchandise options, results in some over-the-top fun collectibles.

My friend Shelly (Kim), one of the best merchandisers *ever*, was working with Tokyo Disney Resort shortly after we met. Through our friendship, I learned that even in merchandising, storytelling is key—even mission critical—because merchandise must continue the story authentically. It has to pass the sniff test. Which leads me to the "Pooh Perfume" controversy. Turns out that there was a line of character perfumes for sale at Tokyo Disney Resort. One of the top sellers was Pooh Perfume. (Or was it called "Eau de Pooh"?) Apparently some cultural misunderstanding allowed its creation, and the name's double meaning made it a scent-sation. But keepers of character stories cried "foul." And rightly so. Pooh Perfume was removed from the shelves without delay, restoring peace to the Hundred Acre Wood and ensuring that Winnie the Pooh would stay true to his essence, forever smelling as sweet as honey.

Branding Is What You Do to Cattle

In the mid-to-late 1990s, Disney financial analysts were concerned with some alarming trends. Revenues were down in consecutive years. Walt Disney Animation Studios hadn't replicated its string of 1989–90s blockbusters—from *The Little Mermaid* to *Beauty and the Beast*, *Aladdin*, and *The Lion King* (although Disney's Pixar partnership had also produced computer-animated blockbusters). And the theme parks, our greatest revenue producer, had suffered declining attendance. An unflattering summary by AdNet.com put it this way, "By the end of the 1990s a good deal of the shine had come off the company's prestige."[5] More inflammatory was the commentary of two investment analysts who wrote, "Disney is a bloated consumer discretionary mutual fund peddling every type of entertainment product conceivable. We do not believe that Disney's new brands/businesses will last and/or be highly exploitable." They did concede one enduring strength. "There is one tiny but powerful presence that has withstood the test the time . . . the mouse."[6]

Company discussions centered on a related concern. We were missing the next generation of Disney fans. Sure, younger audiences were familiar with our animated movies, beginning with *The Little Mermaid*, but it seemed the next generation didn't know or relate to Disney and especially the characters that had started it all—the Fab Five: Mickey, Minnie, Donald, Pluto, and Goofy. How would we appeal to a teenage audience? Everyone wanted to make sure we didn't miss a key demographic that could one day materialize as a shrinking Disney fan base. The goal was to make "cradle-to-grave" Disney fans across theme parks, movies, television, and merchandise. Some believed the best way to attract this new generation of prospective Disney fans was to reshape our nostalgic, fairy-tale identity and "edge up." (And I wondered, what exactly does *that* mean? Make the Disney brand "edgy"?)

Against this backdrop, Roy called and asked if I would meet with him to discuss "the *brand*." I loved any opportunity to be with Roy because he knew better than anyone the heart of Disney. And he always had great stories to share about Uncle Walt and Disney's early days.

On the appointed day, I entered Roy's office, itself a treasure with memorabilia from his dad and uncle and on the walls, photos of his boat the *Pyewacket,* one of his great loves. I had barely sat down when he said, "Jody, you know branding is something you do to cattle." He smiled and with a wink continued to tell me that Disney is not a brand. It will never be a brand. And we will never just put a stamp on the outside of the organization to define it. Instead, we must pledge to stay committed to Disney's core, which will always emanate from the inside out.

He believed branding involved tagging something on the outside, affixing some identity-of-the-month, and hoping it would stick. Roy was committed to managing something of lasting value. He wanted Disney to be pure at its core and not lose its way with gimmicks or quick fixes that might appeal to a broader audience initially, but ultimately could devalue the essence of the company that bore his name—Disney. Roy was concerned that all this "tinkering with so-called brand issues" might lead to changes that would jeopardize Disney's reputation and even its existence.

At a well-publicized and contentious annual shareholders' meeting in 2003, Roy addressed the crowded ballroom on the topic:

> In recent times, there's been a tendency to refer to it as the "Disney brand." To me, this degrades Disney into a "thing" to be bureaucratically managed, rather than a "name" to be creatively championed. And lately I've been seeing Mickey receive this treatment too, as well as Pooh and a lot of others . . . .
>
> The Walt Disney Company is more than just a business. It is an authentic American icon—which is to say that over the years it has come to stand for something real and

meaningful and worthwhile to millions of people of all ages and backgrounds around the world.[7]

Your Brand Is Your Promise

Despite his disdain for the "branding" buzzword, Roy instinctively knew what skilled brand stewards preach—and practice: Your brand is your promise. It's the pledge that the Disney you meet in the movies or at an Epcot attraction or in an exchange with Mary Poppins on Main Street, U.S.A. in Disneyland Paris, is the same. *It's us, Disney. You know us!* In fact, it's the people who experience Disney who best express what Disney is. Because in the end, you don't define your brand. The people who know you and interact with you do.

This is what Roy was talking about. At that now historic meeting, he also said:

> I believe our mission has always been to be bringers of joy, to be affirmers of the good in each of us, to be—in subtle ways—teachers. To speak, as Walt once put it, "not to children but to the child in each of us."
>
> We do this through great storytelling, by giving our guests a few hours in another world where their cares can be momentarily put aside, by creating memories that will remain with them forever. This is the core of what we've come to call "Disney," and to my mind, our single biggest need is to get back to that core.[8]

Bingo, Roy. Nothing edgy about that.

The Core

So how do you discover what's at the core of your organization, your family, or even yourself? No surprise, I found the answer back on the family farm.

One of the best ways to reveal what's inside is to add light. I mentioned earlier that my dad was born and raised on an Indiana farm. When our family visited the farm, we would help with the daily chores. One of my favorites was candling the eggs. With Grandma Carbiener, a talented organist and lifelong learner who married into farm life, I would gather the eggs from the chicken coop into a basket and then carry them down into the cellar. One by one we would hold the eggs up to the light to see if there were any impurities in the egg. If there were, we couldn't sell them.

Amazing how God uses light in many forms for our benefit. Light is the source of vitality, nourishment, direction, and truth. When we work up the courage to hold our lives (or life's work) up to the light, we begin to see where we are living outside of an authentic core. Impurities become visible and, often, regrettable.

Discovering the core may require even more, including the arduous work of removing the dingy, scarred coatings disguising the essence underneath. When my husband, John Dreyer, and I set about refinishing the long-neglected floors in our new home, we sanded them down to the grain. I wondered how we would know when we had sanded enough but not too much to damage the core. Every expert we talked to said we'd just know. We'd stop when we unmasked the "heart" of the wood. You know, they were right. And it was worth the hard work to get to the true beauty within.

Integrity

Once you've discovered your core (whether as a person, family, or global organization), you uncover the promise you are uniquely equipped to make. *Keeping* that promise, over and over in every encounter, develops brand integrity. What does the word *integrity* mean to you? To me it means wholeness, "the state of being whole and undivided." In my mind, nothing matters more. What if, instead of managing a brand, we cultivated integrity? And not an easy, on-the-surface fix like sticking plastic flowers in an untilled field and expecting them to smell sweet. But the harder work of preparing soil, planting seeds, tending, feeding, pruning, and awaiting a harvest that can only flourish from the inside out.

The importance of cultivating integrity can't be underestimated. Harvard Business School professor Michael Jensen says plainly (sounding a little like Roy) that without integrity "nothing works." He claims that by practicing integrity, or more specifically by "respecting the law of integrity," a business can improve productivity by as much as 500 percent. What? He says the rewards of being a person of integrity are just as profound. Jensen wrote this—in plain English, by the way, which I love: ". . . we define integrity for an individual, group, or organization as: honoring one's word. Oversimplifying somewhat, 'honoring your word,' as we define it, means you either keep your word, or as soon as you know that you will not, you say that you will not be keeping your word to those who were counting on your word and clean up any mess you caused by not keeping your word."[9]

Elsewhere Jensen writes simply, "Who I am is my word."

Who are you? What is your state of being? Do you know? Have you ever had that discussion—*before* the meeting on new logos and campaigns? The hard work starts there. Because what's inside will always come out.

Inside Out

No matter how hard you try or how much money you spend to create a sparkly new exterior, time and circumstance eventually reveal essence. While I have nothing against sparkly exteriors, they're tough to maintain. On the other hand, a sparkle from within lit by living with integrity is not so easily extinguished.

I'm not saying we shouldn't question, change, or try new things, or that we'll never make a mistake. In our meetings, inevitably someone would ask, "What would Walt say?" or "What would Walt do?" The one person who never asked that question was Roy. He would respond to those questions this way: "The one thing I know Uncle Walt would do is push boundaries, try new things, utilize any new technology available to us to be on the forefront of creativity."

But pushing creative boundaries is vastly different from "edging up." Does Disney strike you as edgy? When I think "edgy," I picture a middle-aged torso in a crop top. As Roy once said, "This doesn't work." Agreed. I would add, what's inside eventually comes out.

And yet there's still great news. Change is possible. We all know people, organizations, and brands that have transformed. And this kind of growth and brand building done from the inside out is fun and comparatively easy—*so much easier* than squeezing into a look or an identity that just doesn't fit no matter how far you stretch the fabric of believability.

Transformation is a possibility Disney celebrates and an eternal theme that speaks to a longing of the heart of so many Disney fans. I count myself among them. I think that's behind the enduring popularity of *Beauty and the Beast*. As the Beast transformed, we had a front row seat to a miraculous event. The Beast's animator felt the same way.

Glen was inspired by the spiritual truth in the love story between Belle and the Beast. The very premise of the tale is that appearances can be deceptive. Beauty is found within. The Beast's exchanges with the beggar woman, and later with Belle, cast light on his inner nature but also hint at the possibility of transformation. Glen animated what's possible when love exposes our innate self-centeredness and propels us to change. In the film's mesmerizing transformation sequence, we witness what happens when the Beast becomes a prince—from the inside out.

In this, my friend also depicted the *process* of transformation—the reckoning with our brokenness (like examining our core in the light), and because of grace gently offered, a yielding to the loving and ongoing restoration of our hearts. In the Beast, the wind powers the change. "To me," Glen said, "the wind is like the spirit of God that does this transformation in our lives."[10]

In 2002 the Library of Congress entered the Academy Award-winning *Beauty and the Beast* into its National Film Registry because it was a "culturally, historically, or aesthetically significant" film. It could have been included for its captivating expression of truth applicable to organizations and individuals alike: Beauty—and integrity—come from within.

THE HEART OF DISNEY

At the same time that the inner offices of Disney were talking about "edging up," the idea of reissuing Disney's classic animated films in new formats to speak to new audiences was born. And so began the process of delivering the beloved stories via cutting-edge technologies and channels. Films were remastered and reissued on VHS tape, and then on DVD and later Blu-Ray. Today Disney classics enter and come out of "The Vault" in platinum and diamond editions and signature collections with added content and new technology (like app-accessible interactive trivia and sing-along elements) to engage new viewers.

In a similar way, Disney embarked on extending its stories. The modern classic *The Lion King* was the source of direct-to-video sequels, a television series, video games, books, and the wildly successful (pun intended) Broadway musical. The delivery mechanisms have changed, but the characters and fairy-tale heart of the content has not. New generations are meeting The Walt Disney Company—the real Disney—and falling in love the way their parents and grandparents did.

Most recently, Disney created a product in an old language for a new audience of native Navajo speakers. Pixar's *Finding Nemo* has been dubbed in Navajo so that Nemo fans and guardians of a vanishing language can enjoy the film and preserve a treasure at the same time. I feel certain this is the kind of project Walt would delight in. Whether in English, Czech, Spanish, or Navajo, the film speaks fluent Disney. As Walt himself said:

I think we have made the fairy tale fashionable again. That is, our own blend of theatrical mythology. The fairy tale of film—created with the magic of animation—is the mode equivalent of the great parables of the Middle Ages. Creation is the word. Not adaptation. Not version. We can translate the ancient fairy tale into its mode equivalent without losing the lovely patina and the savor of its once-upon-a-time quality. I think our films have brought new adult respect for the fairy tale. We have proved that the age-old kind of entertainment based on the classic fairy tale recognizes no young, no old.[11]

Walt Disney

CHAPTER 4

STORY

Yours Matters. Tell It Well.

Princess or pixie, prince or beast, there's always more to the story. Understanding a person from the inside out doesn't happen without getting at that story. I often use STORY as an acronym to remind myself of this: **S**tories **T**ell **O**thers about the **R**eal **Y**ou. At Disney, discovering and revering story—and the real you and me—happens everywhere and every day, from elaborate stage productions to something as simple as a name tag.

The first and most treasured of my name
tags with dozens more to follow.

Disney issues name tags in the tens of thousands to employees (or "cast members"), engraved with their first names (only) along with a hometown, college, or country. Why? The name tags invite connection and conversation with guests. And using first names makes the interaction friendlier. Disney encourages these connections because the greatest storytelling company ever *never* forgets that every cast member and every guest has a story.

One blogger has compiled links to more than 640 blog sites dedicated exclusively to Disney World. Every half hour the site is updated with the most recent posts from Disney World loyalists. And you can find other blogs written by self-described Disney fanatics and geeks on anything and everything Disney. These are my people! There are multigenerational stories like those shared on growingupdisney.com, describing the author's earliest memories of Disney World when he visited the preview center in an Orlando orange grove. Or the young mama of three boys who says she's always planning a trip to Disney even if they never quite happen. These brides, moms, foodies, photographers, artists, and everyday fans have something to say. Every guest has a story worth telling.

And so do you.

Not only that, but you are telling your story every day. Whether about the business you represent, the faith you hold dear, the food you're passionate about, the politics you favor, the sports teams you cheer, or the people you live with and love, you're telling a tale that more than ever before—like it or not—may have a permanent record. (Call it your digital footprint, which sounds a little fleeting to me when it's more like a footprint in Walk of Fame cement.) The media available to us not only amplify and disperse our messages, but to some extent they catalog our life. I think of these media as personal billboards, except where we once could take down a message we regret, we no longer have that option. The Cloud has a long memory.

Now, we could overthink this new reality to the point of paralysis. We could become too fearful to go anywhere, to do or to ~~say~~ post anything. On the other hand, we could walk carelessly through each day, sending out communications that don't represent our truer selves. I think there's a middle ground we can find with a little intentionality.

Folks would do well to think about marketing and promoting their personal story with the same diligence as businesses do. That idea may seem foreign, even slightly distasteful. Self-promotion? Sales? Marketing . . . me and my life? It sounds disingenuous, doesn't it? Well, how about taking some of the muck and mystery out of the term *marketing* by thinking of it as *messaging*, or even *narrative* or *storytelling*.

Okay, let's stop here. Even if we cleared the marketing and self-promotion hurdle, I can imagine you thinking, *This isn't for me. I might have a story, but I don't need to tell it especially well. I'm not selling anything. No one really cares. Besides, it's my story. Whether I tell it well or not, it won't matter to anyone else.* Really? While I won't say you're wrong (not in so many words anyway), I will ask you to hear me: *Your story matters*! Disney's John (Lasseter) has said, "Your voice is worthwhile; have faith in it." I couldn't agree more. I have no doubt that just as story itself has the power to change the characters we meet in Disney films, your voice—your story—also has the power to change the lives of people around you. *Your story matters.*

And who knows your story better than you? Whether you work in or own a business, whether you advocate for a nonprofit, coach a team, or manage a smaller organization called a family, you are both a story keeper and a storyteller. Your life is your story. And if you don't tell your story, others will. Don't consign your story to careless messages and uninformed opinions. Message and narrate your story in a way that honors it. Talk about your successes and breakthroughs, as well as your breakdowns and stumbles in a way that celebrates the divine purposes of plot twists in your own epic tale.

What's the Heart of Your Story?

Businesses known for excellence in marketing know their story. And then they develop proficiency in telling it every day to audiences that matter to them. As we talked about earlier, the linchpin in this practice is knowing the heart of the brand and what sets it apart. Disney "creates happiness by providing the finest in entertainment for people of all ages, everywhere."[1] Simply put. Disney has forged its sterling reputation through the consistent delivery of that promise in every experience with every Disney business unit from consumer products to theme parks to movies.

One way to discover the overarching theme of your story is by considering how others describe you (personally, or the business or organization you represent). What is your reputation? Or maybe your nickname? Do the key characters in your life— your colleagues, family members, and friends—refer to you as detail-oriented, visionary, a nature lover, full of compassion, hardworking, or encouraging? Knowing yourself (princess or pixie?) is key to building your story and developing your central theme. This isn't something you necessarily think about or rehearse every day, but businesses, churches, families, and individuals all need to summarize that one-of-a-kind narrative and get to the very *heart* of their story. Boil this all down to two or three sentences that express the core of what you want people to know and think about you and hopefully to pass along.

Here again, I imagine you thinking, *Hopefully pass along? Um, I think I mentioned before, I'm not selling anything.* Oh, but you are. Maybe you're not selling something, but you are broadcasting what drives you all the time. And people notice.

So, Here's My Story (Eyes Wide Open)

Years ago it was common knowledge that the adult attention span was roughly twelve minutes. This explains why television programs were interrupted with commercials near the twelve-minute mark. Thanks to advanced technology, so they say, that window has closed to about five minutes. More recent research suggests we might actually have the attention span of a goldfish—clocking in at about nine seconds.[2] (And for me, sometimes even that feels like an eternity.) That's not much time to broadcast your essential message. Imagine how photos, posts, and tweets begin to shape your story. It ups the ante for organizations and for individuals too, who want to craft an accurate account of who they are and what they are about. Your "digital life" won't be perfect. Just let the true you come out.

When Disney Animation began work on *The Lion King*, the core theme was, by most accounts, a little muddled. As the studio's first movie to feature an original storyline and not an adaptation of a classic tale, it was equal parts National Geographic nature film and *Hamlet* meets *Bambi*. Originally called *King of the Jungle*, it was sometimes referred to as *Bambi in Africa*, or sometimes just *Bamblet*. But eventually, and not without a little struggle, the story's creators discovered its identity as a coming-of-age story rooted in a father-son relationship. It speaks to the process of assuming your responsibilities and destiny in the great circle of life. In layer upon layer, the film developed from that proposition. Every word from the scriptwriters' text, each of the (literally) million drawings of six hundred artists, animators, and technicians, every note that Elton John or Hans Zimmer composed, and every line from lyricist Tim Rice supported the core theme.[3] And following in vital supporting roles, the movie trailer, press releases, expert interviews, and promotional messages contributed to the narrative. Theme park attractions, consumer products, video games, and DVD bonus features continue the tale only because the story's foundation is secure.

Once you've established the premise of your story and considered all of the messaging that supports it, you have to know yourself well enough to guard against straying off message or losing your way. *Focus* is the key to maintaining your storyline. Remember how Disney had to settle on the definition of a princess and make sure they were portraying the princesses in ways that were consistent with their storylines? We had to stop sending mixed messages to our audience and realign our efforts.

Another example of focusing on story integrity comes from Disney's theme parks. If you have visited any one of them, you may have noticed that you never see a cast member in a Jungle Cruise costume walking down Main Street or a hostess in a Fantasyland costume running Star Tours in Tomorrowland. Disney guards the consistency of its messaging. Disney appreciates what it means to be coherent and completely committed to a storyline, so much so that it syncs its message with its image and experience anywhere you connect with The Walt Disney Company. With a few exceptions and the occasional misstep, Disney keeps its promise. We should too.

A Fractured Fairy Tale

Did you know that *The Lion King*, the highest grossing two-dimensional film ever, was once considered a B project? It was secondary at the time to *Pocahontas*, a project more in the tradition of *The Little Mermaid*, *Beauty and the Beast*, and *Aladdin* that was expected to be the next blockbuster. Creative mastermind Don (Hahn) was brought into the project when he had finished *Beauty and the Beast*. And at the same time, it was decided to make *Bamblet* a musical. Don said of the "B-team" talent under his direction: "I suppose the biggest thing I learned was that even though it was the B-movie and nobody wanted to work on it and it was seen as the step-child, to never count a project out until it's done because you never know."[10] The artists working on *The Lion King* may have been a little young and untested, but then again, so was Simba.

Do you ever consider yourself "B" talent, starring in your own subpar movie? Keep at it. Trust the process. Remember, a great story involves conflict and challenges, plot twists and turns. As Don might say, don't count yourself out too soon. The final chapter of your story has yet to be written.

Shape Your Story (Ears Attuned)

Along with knowing yourself, you must also know your audience and tailor your story accordingly. You do that by listening and learning. Here again, if you're not convinced you have a story, you may not believe you have an audience. But you do. Your coworkers hear you on the phone and in meetings. Your committee members listen to your input. Your spouse probably knows your essential message well enough to repeat your lines. And if you have children in your home, you have a captive audience. They are listening and, maybe more convicting, they're watching—3D glasses firmly in place.

I am not suggesting you cater to the characters around you in a way that would be inconsistent with who you are. That would be like stripping Tink of her tunic and corseting her in a ball gown just because a few Disney fans like taffeta and silk. But you can shape your message, recognizing that one size rarely fits all. In the 1980s, Disney theme parks joined with noted travel writer Steve Birnbaum to create the Birnbaum Disney Travel Guides. Birnbaum's first publication was actually a one-size-fits-all solution: *The Birnbaum Guide to Walt Disney World*. The idea was that since Disney parks are designed to entertain people of all ages, we needed only one guide for every reader. However, as we studied our audience, we learned that a significantly large segment thought the parks were for kids, not kids *and* adults (or as Disney likes to think of them, kids of all ages).

So a few years later, under the ever-intelligent leadership of my friend Wendy (Lefkon), Disney and Birnbaum began publishing *Birnbaum's Walt Disney World without Kids* and *Birnbaum's Dining Guide*. In addition, the parks began to message differently to their varied audiences. Wendy understood how to speak directly to targeted audiences with relevant and engaging content. Disney didn't change its entertainment, its venues, or its core message. We simply realized that there was not a single-size delivery that fit all audience segments. My pal Linda (Warren), ever the strategic guru, was also at work identifying the unique interests of our guests so we could speak more personally to each group. Today that message is also delivered digitally, allowing the reader to customize their Disney information download and "self-segment." Regardless of the delivery mechanism, all of the communications from Disney to groups like Intenders (those who want to visit) or Disneyphiles (those who visit regularly) support the premise that Disney theme parks are the happiest places on earth, offering the finest in family entertainment for people of all ages.

Here's another way to think about it. If you're committed to your message, you need to consider the folks you interact with every day in the way an ambassador would get to know a host country and its citizens. In what language and with what affect will you communicate most effectively? There are five questions you should ask yourself, and these apply whether you are drafting prepared remarks for a company meeting or chatting with friends and acquaintances:

- What does the audience want? What are their interests or goals? (You find the answers to these questions by first being a great listener.)

- What do I want my audience to know? (What is the news I have to share?)

- What is the audience's likely attitude about my message?

Q How can I honor my audience's needs and perspectives?

Q What do I have to say that might surprise and delight my audience?

So now let's check the boxes. You know yourself. (Eyes wide open.) You've discovered your audiences and their needs by listening to them. (Ears attuned.) Now you're ready to express your essential message. (Mouth moving.) Wait—maybe not so fast. What are you saying?

Let's take a look at what I call the magic keys to messaging. And by the way, if you scan this list of how-to's and think they must only apply to the business world, hang in there. You'll see how these keys apply just as well to your own personal story.

How Should I Say . . . ? (Mouth Moving)

When you care deeply about your message, it's worth pausing to consider a few communication tips. You know, tips to help listeners "C" what you're saying.

Communicate clearly. As my husband would say: "Mean what you say and say what you mean." If your audience doesn't understand what you are saying, you're missing an opportunity. Be clear about what you are saying by using the language or terminology your listeners understand. If you don't say what you mean in your audience's language, you could wind up like Kentucky Fried Chicken when it entered the Chinese market. To its horror (and probably more horrifying to its dining public), KFC discovered its slogan "finger lickin' good" had been translated "Eat your fingers off." In a similar way, the Coca-Cola Company message was misrepresented in China (mostly by shopkeepers) with a phonetic translation of its name. The localized translations meant something like "bite the wax tadpole." Eventually the company landed on an official trademark expressed in Mandarin characters "K'o K'ou K'o Lê," meaning "Let your mouth rejoice."[4] Now that's saying what you mean.

*C*ommunicate convincingly. The plain and simple truth is that if you're not excited about what you're saying, then you cannot communicate in a compelling way. I would add that if you don't balance your enthusiasm with the facts and information that ground your message in truth, your passion won't win the day. Most decisions involve both the head and heart. So provide the information someone needs to legitimize a decision, but remember that people respond to passion, because "the heart has its reasons which reason does not know."[5]

*C*ommunicate creatively. When Donald Duck turned fifty, Disney was faced with the anniversary of yet another character and the challenge of distinguishing the milestone within its parade of annual commemorations. Publicity head and Disney legend, Charlie (Ridgway), concocted a scheme—or maybe I should say he hatched a plan. With Disney's curator of Discovery Island, he arranged for the incubation of fifty Peking duck eggs. When the eggs hatched, the first thing the hatchlings saw was the theme park version of Donald Duck. To reinforce the bond, the ducklings were fed daily by cast members in Donald's costume. The plan was for Donald's ducks to follow him in the Magic Kingdom's daily parade that summer. Charlie collaborated with

Disney's theme park costumers to make birthday hats and Disney name tags for each of the Peking ducks to wear in the parade. Yes, each duck had its own name. But for a minor mishap when the fifty ducklings waddled out of parade formation to take a dip in the castle moat, the plan worked (and was perfected when they were safely corralled on a float) and the word spread far and wide (even appearing in *Life* magazine) that Donald was turning fifty.

Now, I know you might not have all of Disney's resources. But you have the most important one: imagination! The Donald Duck example worked for Disney because it is an entertainment company. You can come up with ideas big and small that work perfectly for you. The unexpected notion can catapult into a big idea in your messaging. (Oh, and just in case you wondered, once the party was over, the birthday ducks were given in pairs to zoos around the country.

Susan and Louise on Donald Duck's fiftieth birthday tour. Getting their ducks in a row was never more challenging.

The always enthusiastic and engaging Susan (Hartnett), then Walt Disney World Ambassador, presented these quacking party favors. What stories she has about her duck deliveries!)

*C*ommunicate consistently and coherently. Your storytelling can and ought to be as fresh and creative as duck hatchlings, but your core message should remain the same today and tomorrow as it was yesterday, and that message ought to be demonstrated by your actions, consistently and coherently. For example, did you know that in Disney's theme parks there are no lost children? Only lost adults. When cast members discover a child whose parents have wandered off, or when a parent reports a child at large, cast members call in a "Signal 70." Innocuous, nothing to alarm the child—or the parent. Word goes out across the park to be on alert for an unaccompanied child. Once found, the cast member discovering the child befriends the young guest. By the time the parents and child are reunited, the young guest has had a pretty great time making a new friend. Even in an "emergency" like this, Disney park cast members continue to communicate a story (and experience) that results in a happy ending. Disney's story would be compromised if a place designed for children somehow incited panic, or inflicted some sort of punishment for something that we all know happens with kids and crowds. What you say should always align with what you do, because well done always trumps well said. That's more or less how a blogger described her Signal 70 experience: "When I arrived at Big Thunder Mountain Railroad, my Lost Boy was happily chatting with his new friend, but he was thrilled to see his mom and I was thrilled to see him. The cast member was extremely complimentary of how responsible and calm he had been through the process, and even she seemed relieved that we were reunited. Like everything else, Disney does finding lost children with excellence." (So excellent in fact, that the blogging mom didn't even realize that she had been the one who was lost!)

*C*ommunicate contagiously. One of the best ways to get information out about your essential message is through others. Every day you send out "agents," people telling stories about you, your business, or your nonprofit. Your patrons, coworkers, neighbors, and friends should be your communication allies. Like it or not, they are already telling stories about you. Some of that buzz is old school communication—just talk. And a lot of it is by way of social media, which is word of mouth in the digital age. The challenge you face is making your key message a part of someone else's storytelling. To do so, you have to make sure they are aware of the good stories they can be telling about you. And the best stories are those that are contagious—spread virally, person-to-person or across social media.

To illustrate, Walt Disney's first movie publicist was a man named Eddie (Meck). Said to have been diminutive in stature with ears like Mickey Mouse, he stands tall in Disney's history. His mantra was, "We can perform every trick in the book to open a movie. But the film is going to succeed or fail because of what the people who see this movie have to say about it to their friends." Eddie realized nothing makes for a better story than personal experience. When Disneyland opened, Eddie figured an advertisement or press release in the newspaper would be a poor substitute for an actual park experience. As a result, much of Disneyland's opening publicity centered on personal contact with the press and inviting them to experience Disneyland for themselves. He said he couldn't promote the park like they had the movies. "It's just so different and nobody's going to believe what we're telling them." When Walt asked what the solution was, Eddie said, "I'm going to get them to see for themselves." Eddie also said, "If you have a good product, it's easy to get the message across. No gimmicks. Just truth and honesty. The greatest product is right here: Walt Disney."[6]

What is more valuable to you in choosing a dentist, a restaurant, a movie, or a vacation experience? Is it an ad, or is it the recommendation made by someone you know? That's the power of word of mouth. Harness it. Cultivate it. And most of all, cherish it!

Communicate in community. Your story will be stronger if it's created in community with the advocacy and input of people you trust. Who are your advocates? Who are the people with influence in the community who support you and the work that you do? Identify them and seek their help. Their energy and credibility may provide a needed "halo effect."

When Disney was planning its Animal Kingdom theme park, criticism about Disney's ability to handle live animals began to bubble up. Disney, responding to the sage advice of my husband (then head of corporate communications) and others, realized there was a key planning and messaging element missing. To make sure the team was designing the park correctly and with integrity, we recognized the need to assemble an outside advisory committee of noted animal experts. These experts could provide valuable input on animal care and address criticism as well. The committee issued creative and practical input to the park's final design and messaging. And because they were vested in the project and believed it was being executed the right way, they became some of the park's strongest advocates and fiercest defenders.

This is an encouragement to invite others' opinions. Don't be afraid to incorporate their ideas and input, even when the input comes from surprising places. Consider this: Disney sent a team of animators from *The Lion King* to Western Africa to study the animals and environment. They later took all the animators to the San Diego Zoo and Wild Animal Park to study the animals' movement and behavior for longer periods of time. Then the team invited Jim Fowler, known for his television show *Wild Kingdom*, to bring live adult lions into the animators' studio. As if that weren't enough, the producers asked an animal anatomy specialist to lecture about bone and muscle structure. That degree of input made for a movie filled with believable images—a good story well told.

Communicate courageously. What do you do when your messages go rogue? When unplanned circumstances interrupt your best laid plans? Be courageous. Seize the opportunity to turn unplanned events into positives that communicate an unvarnished truth about who you are and what you do. Speak truth.

Walt Disney World once operated a bird sanctuary called Discovery Island. It was a habitat for birds of all kinds, including an emu that one day plucked a large diamond ring off of a guest's finger. (Don't ask me how!) The bird proceeded to swallow it. The island's curator had an idea of how to retrieve the ring and thought it might make for a good story. He contacted the publicity department, which developed a humorous piece about the thieving bird and the "heroic and magical" efforts to reclaim the ring and return it to its rightful owner. The story reinforced the "Happiest Place on Earth" narrative where magical experiences happen every day. The media saw a good human interest story and ran with it. Disney recognized that when the unexpected happens, with awareness and a bit of humor, you might find a diamond in the droppings.

And that's the truth, isn't it? Things happen. Sometimes in spite of your efforts, and sometimes because of them. We all make mistakes and say or do things that fill us with regret. But I also know that our mistakes and regrets are redeemable. I have learned the place of our deepest pain can become the place of our greatest connection and service to others.

Communicate to connect. Speaking of redeeming pain, let's revisit *The Lion King*. Remember when Simba comes face-to-face with the memory of his father, when he has to grapple with his culpability and shame? Without anger or reproach, Mufasa says, "You are more than what you have become. . . . Remember who you are." That scene has connected powerfully with movie-and theater-goers alike. Don (Hahn), the movie's esteemed producer, said the most surprising reactions from the movie have been the emotional ones, like a weeping woman who thanked him for making the movie because it helped her grieve her father's death and frame that great loss in her life. That wasn't the outcome Don expected when they were creating the movie, but it shows how our stories (and our authenticity) can connect us in ways that can bring healing and wholeness. And this is how communication is not just about business, but can change *your* story.

Write Your Happy Ending First

Maybe you'd be more courageous in your storytelling if you knew how your story would end. Well, try this on for size. How's the story gone so far? Think back to a place where you felt lost or confused, a place where you struggled personally or professionally. Did anything about your story make sense to you when you were in the middle of it? But what about now? Can you see where your struggle was necessary or where confusion led to clarity? Sometimes our stories make more sense when we read them backward, when we see how many scenes that seemed painful or even unimportant at the time foreshadowed something of life-changing significance. I tend to believe that nothing in our story is wasted, and looking back can help us move forward—as long as we don't try to drive by looking in the rearview mirror.

I also believe we ought to think about the end of our story. What will "happily ever after" mean for you? I know lots of people wouldn't think of reading the end of the book first. No way! But I came across a little research revealing that reading ahead to the story's last chapter doesn't spoil the ending. Not at all. It enhances it. The University of California, San Diego researchers put it this way: "Reading a spoiled story is analogous to driving to a known destination. The driver may be less concerned about the exact nature of the destination and how to interpret signs along the way, and therefore be more free to enjoy the scenery and other incidental pleasures."[7] When you know the story ends well, you can enjoy its unfolding along the way. Plot twists become less frightening. The mundane has a purpose. The simple becomes sacred. And you can believe that every word moves you toward your own happily ever after.

My family's favorite coach is the legendary John Wooden. He was from my mom's Indiana hometown and was an All-American basketball player at Purdue. Most notably, he was the winning and revered UCLA basketball coach. He lived a life of deep faith that, in part, was shaped by a seven-point creed given to him by his dad. Third on that list is this charge: "Make each day your masterpiece."[8] If that is your motto, your story will end well. And, remember, if somehow the ending seems hopeless or painful, it's likely not the end of the story—just the end of a chapter.

CIRCLE OF TRUST

I referred to John Lasseter earlier. He is the genius (and boundlessly energetic) chief creative officer for Disney and Pixar animation and Disney's Imagineering as well. At Pixar, John participated in something brilliant called the "Braintrust." Begun during the making of *Toy Story*, it was the periodic gathering of creatives—usually movie directors and writers—to provide feedback on a movie in development. The "notes" given within the group were not dictates, just an offer of candid commentary from other storytellers. The meetings helped take films from mediocre to meteoric.

When John and Pixar joined the Disney family, he instituted the same kind of gatherings for Disney animated films and called it the "Story Trust." I think we ought to have the same sort of group in our personal lives. Maybe call it your "Circle of Trust." My friend and co-writer, Stacy, has a group of friends (former high school classmates) who are just that. For twenty-four consecutive years, they have met to spend a long weekend to speak into each other's lives. It's not set up that formally, but the result is the same. Over the course of four days, all eight of them share what's going on in their lives, and they receive each other's advice, affirmation, love, and support. Because these friends know each other's histories and hopes, each one is a trusted voice in the understanding of the past and the composition of the chapter yet to be written. Authentic storytelling can be messy and often scary. Bréne Brown has said, "Owning our story and loving ourselves through that process is the bravest thing we will ever do."[9] Your Circle of Trust can be the safe space to own and share the story of the real you.

CHAPTER 5

CHARACTERS
The People We Love Will Change Us

It may have started with a mouse—almost named Mortimer, by the way (nice save by Walt's wife, Lillian)—but imagine if Disney had fixated on one character. Only one. Or imagine if Walt had convinced himself that he alone could animate a mouse named Mickey and entertain generations of story lovers by himself and with his talents alone. Not a chance. And Walt knew that. He said, "You can dream, create, design, and build the most wonderful place in the world but it requires people to make the dream a reality."[1] (Interesting, isn't it, that in the garden of Eden—the original theme park with unparalleled adventure, beauty, food, and fun—"it was not good" for man to be alone.) If paradise was incomplete without companionship, then even the Happiest Place on Earth would disappoint without its diverse cast of characters.

Most of our stories are told like an epic with hundreds in the cast of characters. But in the pivotal chapters, we probably all share some types of characters who move the story to our happily ever after. I'll call those leading characters our friends, fairy godmothers, and fiends.

Of Friends, Fairy Godmothers, and Fiends

Friends—Your Fab Five

Is there a better group of friends than the Fab Five? Walt drew from our common experience of friendship when he created that cohort of pals: Mickey, Minnie, Donald, Goofy, and Pluto. Mickey is, of course, the central character and protagonist, a mouse we can relate to. Walt said, "When people laugh at Mickey Mouse, it's because he's so human; and that is the secret of his popularity."[2] Mickey was likely Walt's alter ego, and Lillian said that the two—mouse and man—grew up together. Mickey gave Disney a voice that still speaks to our culture. And, quite literally, Walt gave voice to Mickey. It's Walt's voice speaking for the mischievous mouse in cartoon shorts through 1946 and then again in the late 1950s in *The Mickey Mouse Club* television series.

Minnie is Mickey's best gal, his damsel in distress, and often his heroine. Mickey meets Minnie in *Steamboat Willie* when the boat's crane retrieves her from the river's shore and deposits her on deck in the ultimate pickup. While Minnie rebuffed his advances early on, Mickey's charm eventually won her over. Fans so often ask if Minnie and Mickey are married. (That's a loaded question, as you'll see.) We settled on this reply: "Mickey and Minnie are eternal sweethearts." But in a lovely postscript, the later voices of Mickey and Minnie, Wayne Allwine and Russi Taylor, were actually married for nearly twenty years until Wayne's death in 2009.

Add to that romantic duo Donald Duck—the irascible, crusty, quacking friend everyone should have in their corner. And what about Goofy? All friend groups need a Goofy—someone who is just fun to be around. The one who laughs a little too loud and trips over his own feet. A larger-than-life character who's game to try just about anything even if he looks a little ridiculous in the process. Goofy combines eagerness with vulnerability and reminds us that we should take our work—but not necessarily ourselves—seriously. When all else fails, just laugh. A lot. *Garwsh*. The last of the Fab Five is Pluto, the only one of the ensemble to walk on all fours, saying nothing, but remaining loyal to Mickey through thick and thin. Pluto is the faithful friend who practices presence and whose presence alone can buoy you. There are many other Disney friends, like Daisy, who makes the group the Sensational Six; Clarabelle Cow; Huey, Dewey, and Louie; Scrooge McDuck; and Max Goof. A colorful variety of friends makes your kingdom come to life.

But about this closer cohort, the Fab Five. Do you have one? I recently read about a study that discovered that even if we count our friends into the hundreds (or thousands!) on Facebook, we're more likely to rely on only four of those friends in crisis. Only four! These are the friends who will go the distance with you. Together, you are the Fab Five.

Fairy Godmothers—Your Fixers

Even with a Fab Five, we may also need a friend who pops in and out of our lives like a personal fairy godmother. In that great scene in *Cinderella*—the "fix-it" scene, where Cinderella suffers a crisis in wardrobe, carriage, and confidence—who floats in but her fairy godmother? Voila! Well, actually, "bibbidi bobbidi boo"! Just a wave of her wand and Cinderella receives everything she needs to make her date with destiny.

Make believe or not, I have found in life some people are "fixers." Undaunted by titanic obstacles, they take stock of the situation and then get on with it. Done! Every team, group, and project needs that person. For me, that person was Virginia (Hough). We called her Virgie. She was one capable, take-charge fairy godmother. When the world around her dissolved to panic, Virgie became calm and laser-focused. If there was a solution to be found, Virgie found it. Before she came to Disney, she coordinated travel for the 1984 Summer Olympic Games in Los Angeles. So, you see, she had prior experience turning pumpkins into coaches and performing assorted minor miracles. She was not the person out front; nonetheless, she may have been the most vital player to our group's success. Virgie has some crazy made-up title like "administrative coordinator of anything and everyone always and forever," but I think it should also be Fairy Godmother. I wish for you that kind of person in your corner, the kind who sprinkles a little goodness wherever they go. Or, even better, maybe *you* are someone else's Virgie, acting on opportunities that only look like emergencies. I would like to be that kind of problem solver, the kind who notices what others don't see, helping to bring order to chaos and beauty from ashes.

Fiends—Your Complicated Foils

Friends and fairy godmothers are welcome in any cast of characters, but a story of any depth includes a fiendish villain or two. As much as we wish it weren't so, we all have a villain to contend with. Let me rethink that. Actually, we don't wish against villains as much as we wish them to be slightly less villainous. Because something about villains fascinates us. And some of the most beloved characters at our theme parks and in our movies are villains. What would be the point of *101 Dalmatians* without Cruella de Vil? (And at what age did you realize that fur-wearing fashionista's name was a play on "cruel devil"? I think I was in my thirties.)

Disney taught me a few things about villains.

* **Hey, they're just doing their job.** Some of our antagonists aren't really bad to the bone; they just have a role to play. A Disney-trained villain might inspire the best in you. Do you have someone on the team (or around the dinner table) who is willing to ask the tough questions? The questions may seem harsh and create a little tension, but if these folks play for the same team, they ultimately want what you do.

* **The most beloved villains are sympathetic characters.** Imagine your favorites. What, really, did they want? Think about the Evil Queen, Maleficent, Cruella, Lostso, Jafar, and Gaston. Respectively, they wanted to be the fairest; the honored guest; the best dressed; the most loved; the all-powerful; and your bicep-bulging, expectorating hero. Haven't we all wanted to be something on that list? Or something like it? In our yearning, often acting out of pride or insecurity, we render ourselves least likely to receive what we want most of all. Cruella, darling, you'd be every bit as fashionable in a down coat—flea-free and warmer too.

* **Hurt people hurt people.** You and I and the people we love may encounter a villain who appears to delight in fiendishness. It could be a bully who seems gratuitously and habitually malicious. In those situations, I try to remember that pain can be referred, and that hurt people often hurt others—even ones they love.

Characters Are Complicated

Disney stories—and our own stories too—start and end with characters. It takes characters of all kinds to make a classic story. Without them, our life has no meaning. That's a lesson I learned over and over again working in and around the castles of Disney. Whether onstage or backstage, characters matter most! And boy, we all know that life lived among all these characters can get *complicated*. My family will tell you that *complicated* is my go-to word to describe well, hmm, complicated people. It's not usually considered a positive word, but I don't consider it a negative word either. Complicated says what's on the surface isn't always what's underneath and that the obvious is never quite that simple.

Let's talk about the complicated characters you should keep in your life—and the ones you shouldn't. Without delving into armchair psychoanalysis, I bet we can agree that there are some characters who are perpetual drains on our storehouses. Whether on our emotional, relational, physical, or financial resources, some folks make so many withdrawals they threaten to take us under, and put us and others in our lives at risk. These are characters we may have to leave behind. During the early development of *Toy Story*, John Lasseter and his team were given the same sort of direction meant to win a new generation of fans. Be edgy. Capture the attention of a worldly, more cynical adult audience. Per dictate, Pixar initially created Woody to be an edgy and snarky bully. But in an early screening, it became clear that mean-spirited Woody was going to sink the film. In an interview, John said, "The characters, especially Woody, were just repellent! Woody was just awful, awful, awful! And I was embarrassed because it wasn't the movie we set out to make." So John's team went back to work.

In a two-week effort to salvage the project, they re-created the movie they had intended to make all along, featuring sympathetic characters in an endearing story about friendship. *Toy Story* would not have become the history-making treasure we know and love had John and his team allowed "edgy Woody" to remain.

God has placed others in our lives whom we can't or shouldn't write out. Think about those who require much of us for a season of life. We pour into these precious ones and willingly draw from the storehouse, trusting that God will supply all we need—for a season. Then there are others who just take a little more from us, not just for a season, but in every season of life. These characters won't bankrupt us and they'd never want to, but, wow, an ongoing relationship with them comes at a cost. Oh, and they aren't leaving. These folks are part of our ensemble cast. Quite possibly, their "abrasiveness"—or that trait that seems like an ongoing irritation— could be the very substance to smooth our rough edges and soften our hearts. These characters for you could be a coworker, boss, in-law, or sibling. When your storyline with them becomes difficult, it helps to remind yourself that everyone has baggage. We love each other well by helping, or accepting the help we need, to unpack it.

In her book *For the Love*, Jen Hatmaker says that this unpacking should start with grace.

> Not superficial, sentimental fluff but the tough, dig-under-the-surface brand. If a difficult relationship is permanent, grace will grease the wheels. Most thorny people are thorny for a reason. It doesn't excuse bad behavior, but understanding early injuries or hidden wounds cushions blows. It's no free pass, but empathy is a powerful tool toward forgiveness and patience. If we must stay the course, compassion helps us weather the road.[3]

Isn't this how a household of servants-turned-serving-pieces were able to love the Beast? Talk about a thorny personality! But Mrs. Potts, Cogsworth, and Lumière knew the heavy sentence that had burdened the Beast, and they pitied him. That compassion fueled their long-suffering service.

We can't pick some of the members of our ensemble cast, like our families or our coworkers, but we can share more of our life with a diverse cast of characters who enrich our lives. Take a good look at everyone around you and consider how they complete your story and how you complete theirs. Remember that characters move in and out of our lives. Some stay for a time, and others through your final scene. And it's because of story—yours and theirs, and the places they intersect—that characters can change.

Captaining the Cruise Line

Disney's cruise line business had a great leader at the helm, a guy named Matt (Ouimet). Though I was never his direct report, I admired him and appreciated his leadership from my vantage point. Matt had a way of empowering the people around him. With high expectations set for everyone, including himself, businesses and initiatives under his authority sailed. Why? Probably because he not only spoke these words, he operated by them: "The biggest thing we can do is develop other leaders . . . all levels of supervisors. It's about high standards, empathy, understanding and knowing how to motivate people. It's about trying to be that leader that you would want to work for."

But before Matt took charge, even before the commissioning of the first ship, the Disney Cruise Line couldn't launch without answering this question: Would the ships have onboard casinos? It was an obvious question to ask. Most cruise lines derive a significant profit from onboard sources like bars and casinos. As I recall (and as the matter was described in the book, *Success Kills: Sidestep the Snares That Will Steal Your Dreams*),[4] the issue was fiercely debated. (Though others say it was never *really* considered.) But I remember proponents on both sides of the question. Most of our strategic and financial executives favored gambling for its profit potential, but many others thought gambling didn't suit Disney's brand of family entertainment. We sat through meetings, debates, analyses, and expert opinion presentations. And more meetings. The deadline approached at twenty-five knots. The ships' designs would either include casinos or not. Passionate and intelligent support came from both sides, but in the end, Disney's leaders didn't take a vote. They made a decision, because that's what good leaders do. They seek input, advice, and as much information as possible. They listen. And they don't make hurried, uneducated decisions. The best leaders make everyone feel they not only have a voice, but that they also have been heard.

Leaders know the loudest voices aren't always right. Numbers don't always paint a complete picture, and majorities don't always rule. Leaders have to make tough calls according to their best judgment, even if that judgment runs counter to popular opinion. As of this writing, you will not find a casino on a Disney cruise ship.

Characters Who Lead

Walt understood that worthy endeavors call for a cast of characters. He also recognized that orchestrating the efforts of diverse casts requires leadership. In other words, every kingdom needs a king. Forget the claims of the personally empowered, self-started, self-motivated, and self-made successes. They are as empty as the four-year-old telling a parent, "You aren't the boss of me." Oh yeah? I am, and you ought to thank me for it. Every kingdom and wunderkind within its walls needs a king. And a successful cast of characters needs someone in authority leading the team.

It's not so much the style of leadership that defines the leaders I admire most. Whether top-down, bottom-up, or leading from the side, successful leaders use a variety of styles. On any given day in your leadership role, you likely employ some or all of the above. Some decisions are delegated, others are issued from above. Some bosses enjoy locking arms and walking side by side, while others just get out of the way and let the magic happen. A good leader will know the style of management that suits the circumstance and cast of characters. What inspires me most in leadership is deeper than method. It has more to do with the individual.

Take Bob (Mathieson), another Disney Legends honoree who was the head of operations for all of the Walt Disney World theme parks. We called him Uncle Bob, but only behind his back. Uncle Bob's crewcut and stature were enough to tell you he led like a commander. He demanded precision and flawless operation, all so that guests could make magical memories. Uncle Bob was both feared and revered. He didn't smile often, so when you got a smile you knew it was earned. (But if you caught him interacting with the guests, especially the kids, you realized his imposing exterior was a thin veneer over a softy's heart.)

I recall one particular event for dignitaries and community leaders in the Magic Kingdom. He had the team walk all the paths the guests might walk in order to see the park as they would. We walked where they would enter and exit, and even walked into and out of the restrooms they would likely use. Then he asked me to memorize the names of all the invited attendees as well as the groups they would be representing, as I would be the one greeting them at the entrance. What Uncle Bob didn't tell me was that he would be by my side. He had my back through the entire event.

If Uncle Bob led as a fastidious military commander, Beth (Black) led as a resourceful den mother. Responsible for a department once called Seminar Productions, Beth would lead by locking arms with her folks and talking them along. She was curious and clever, and she would never utter the words "I don't know" without also saying, "Let's find out." Oh, and did we. There wasn't a person or place she wouldn't approach for an answer, nor an occasion when she wasn't teaching, training, and encouraging by walking alongside her team.

Speaking of teams—one of my favorite bosses (encouraging, effective, and fun) was actually a twosome that worked as one. Lynda (Wilson) and Sandy (Hawkins) in Guest Relations were my first example of a seamless job-sharing partnership. Such partners. You could discuss something with Sandy on a Tuesday afternoon, and Lynda would pick up the conversation, practically midsentence, on Wednesday morning. They reminded me of Chip and Dale carrying each other's load (acorns in their arms), supporting each other in their labors while playfully enjoying each other's company in the process. (By the way, you can tell Chip from Dale by noticing Chip's brown nose like a chocolate "chip." Dale's is red.) Like the energetic chipmunk duo, Lynda and Sandy served each other so the department could thrive. Putting their egos aside, they perfected the art of baton passing so the team could reach the finish line.

And then there was Steve (Burke). Steve was never my immediate boss, but I watched him first as the developer of Disney Stores, later at the helm of Disneyland Paris (then called Euro Disney), and finally at ABC and ESPN. Such a smart leader, without having to convince anyone of that. He was the guy sent in to get the plan, or fix the plan, and ultimately to execute the plan. What I admired about Steve, in addition to the fantastic business successes to his credit, was that people wanted to follow him. Responding to his quiet leadership, cast members working for him wanted to be the best they could be at their respective jobs to help the team soar.

I refer to Bob, Beth, Team Lynda/Sandy, and Steve as "bosses" in the workplace sense of the word, but actually, my earliest memories of faithful leadership are those of my dad, because a leader can be a parent, committee chairman, coach, or anyone else entrusted with authority. No doubt, you're a leader. An influencer of others. Who looks to you for direction, guidance, and mentorship? Somebody does. I've come to believe the most important attributes of effective leaders can be summarized on five fingers.

Number One: Be truthful and honest. I wish I didn't have to start with this because it seems so obvious; really a prequalification. It should go without saying that you can't lead if you can't be trusted. A dishonest king or queen will bring ruin to the kingdom. End of story. There will be no happily ever after for an organization with a dishonest leader.

🖐 **Number Two: Be present and engaged.** At Disney, leaders in operations actively practiced "management by walking around." I love that concept. It is all about being there. You usually work harder when you are noticed and appreciated, and that can only happen if the king or queen leaves the castle. I am not saying that the CEO needs to be omnipresent, but within an organization leaders of any group or division need to be seen by their team regularly, consistently, and noticeably. Now, being present is not being perfect. The greatest lessons I learned from my parents, mentors, bosses, and all those I looked up to were born out of their reactions to imperfection. There is nothing better than a sincere apology and a quick regroup to teach us how to live life—honestly, openly, and with love.

🖐 **Number Three: Be an example and teacher.** Jesus's words in Luke 6:39–40 say it best: "Can the blind lead the blind? Will they not both fall into a pit? The student is not above the teacher, but everyone who is fully trained will be like their teacher." No matter your beliefs, the undeniable truth is that we become like the people who lead us. If you supervise or manage even one person, your influence can be far greater than you imagine.

When I think about the bosses I served under in my twenty-two Disney roles, those I admired most were trash collectors—managers who picked up trash. I will never forget my first area supervisor (three levels of management above me), who came to greet the new interns on our first day of the Disney College Program and take us on a tour. As we were walking down Main Street, he noticed some trash on the pavement ahead.

He picked it up, threw it away, and just kept on talking, never breaking stride. This is something that all levels of management, from hourly cast members to the head of The Walt Disney Company himself, have in common. No one is in a position so lofty that he can't bend low enough to pick up trash. Good leaders speak most eloquently with their lives.

🖐 **Number Four: Be inspirational, encouraging, and enthusiastic.** According to the various definitions of these words, they're all tied together by the fact that they give something, and these things include breath (inspiration), heart (encouragement), and interest (enthusiasm). Inspiration gives license to create and produce. Encouragement gives hope and confidence. And enthusiasm gives an intense and eager interest. Don't we all want our leaders to inspire us to create and encourage us with hope and confidence, all the while being intensely interested in what we're about? Take care not to confuse the delivery of these gifts with the leadership gifts themselves. Some leaders are naturally outgoing and vivacious, while others are quieter in their encouragement.

🖐 **Number Five: Be kind.** The last finger on the hand of a good leader is kindness. At the end of the day (or the shift), we want to know that our leader cares. This is especially true when times are tough. And we know times will be tough, sometimes personally and sometimes professionally. In every challenging situation, a little kindness goes a long way. Where kindness is confused with weakness, leaders may hesitate to soften up, but you can't lead with a closed fist (see chapter 11 for more on this).

Leading for a Lifetime

I can't talk about leadership without talking about my dad and his leadership legacy. He was my earliest example of a leader with a subtle management style. Dad wasn't the picture of an over-the-top animated leader. The man and leader we knew at home was smart and encouraging, and also a man of few words. Though he was soft-spoken and not inclined to dominate a conversation, even after his death, his is still a strong and powerful voice. Even in his absence, I hear him and he leads me. Following his death, my mom received a letter from an engineer who worked for him. In part, it read:

> There are bosses and then there are leaders and Dr. Carbiener was the best leader I had in my entire career. . . . Wayne was one of those rare individuals that had exceptional management and leadership abilities while also possessing kindness, character and you just liked to be around him (especially that fun sarcasm and wit). . . . He didn't talk a lot, but by example, wisely chosen, smart/informed words, and leadership, my life and the world was better because of him.

What Character Will You Choose?

Disney University is Disney's global training program for all of its cast members, providing orientation for new hires and ongoing development for all cast members. The department is the caretaker of Disney terminology, tradition, and lore. Although DU serves all business segments, the vast majority of Disney cast members work in the theme parks, so training is geared more to roles in the parks. In engaging and celebratory ways, DU immerses new cast members in all things Disney—by way of scavenger hunts in the theme parks and friendly forms of initiation. ("Jody, name the seven dwarfs. Go!")

Because Disney values teamwork so highly, one training exercise required new hires to go into the park with cameras and take photos of a handful of characters they most identified with and a few others they didn't. Cast members researched the traits and tendencies of those characters they related to, as well as the qualities of those less like them. Then, in a group, cast members discussed what they admired about the characters and how to spot those qualities in others.

After we defined our characters, we were assembled into teams of the same characters and then given a task to complete. We then re-formed teams with dissimilar characters to accomplish a comparable task. Interestingly, but not a surprise, the most successful teams were also the most diverse.

When I took part in the exercise, I was Happy and Mickey, with a spoonful of Mary Poppins in the mix. This identified me as generally optimistic, fun-loving, given to the fostering of teamwork, and preferring order and straight talk. In the years that followed my orientation, I realized I wasn't locked into a role or typecast in an unchanging identity. I could choose. Happy, Grumpy, Dopey, Sleepy, Sneezy, Bashful, and Doc were characters and also attitudes. And I had the opportunity to pick the one that fit. Every day. Nine out of ten days, I chose Happy. And I still do, remembering that a complex (and complicated) cast makes for a satisfying story.

So make way for Donald Duck and Pluto. Invite Genie and Lumière too. We can accommodate and appreciate Grumpy if we try, especially when we remember we have appeared in the role of Grumpy from time to time. We each embody a small ensemble of characters. And though it's hard to admit, on any given day, we may even play the villain in someone else's story. It helps to remember that our story isn't more important than anyone else's. Being a minor character with a supporting role in someone else's story might be the most fulfilling role of all.

My Disney Sweetheart

My account of Disney characters is incomplete without the story of my favorite Eeyore, aka Donald Duck, aka Jiminy Cricket, aka John Dreyer. We met at the company Christmas party. I actually knew him prior to that, but he claims he doesn't recall it. (Whatever.)

John Dreyer was a publicist working upstairs in City Hall (on Main Street) and I was a tour guide working in the City Hall offices below. I noticed him and the other folks from Publicity and would say hi, but he was shy and usually focused on some "very important work." Fast-forward to the Christmas party where I ran into Mary, my "On Purpose Partners" friend. Her husband, Bill (Tomlinson), golfed with John Dreyer. They introduced us (formally) that night. Mary and Bill are those fun, friendly, fabulous people who have never met strangers. We all got in this *huge* crazy chat, and a friendship was born.

John Dreyer and I were friends for years. (To this day, I call him John Dreyer. I would use John's full name to distinguish him from the other John in the office. Had I known I would marry John Dreyer, I might have called the other John by his full name instead. But I digress. . . .) We had the perfect "on property" friendship, which meant we attended company events, played on the same volleyball team, hosted business functions together, and served as each other's dates whenever the occasion called for one. This went on for years. (Ten to be exact. John Dreyer says eight. Whatever.)

Then it happened. John Dreyer asked me to a movie "off property." It was a Disney movie, of course, but there was no work involved. Not long after, my monthlong assignments in Disneyland Paris required a longer-term transfer overseas. Before I left, he asked me to marry him—a few times—and I declined. Don't ask why. But after my time away in Paris, I realized my error. I called him when I returned to the States eight months later. When he answered the phone, I said, "Yes." Romantically, he replied, "Yes, what?" John Dreyer wasn't convinced my change of heart was a lasting one, so he put me off. Eventually he accepted my marriage reproposal and sent flowers with the message, "Yes, I will marry you." (He holds it over my head that I had to ask him. Again, whatever.) We were married in a small ceremony over the Christmas holidays and announced our marriage in a card that read, "Hope your holidays are filled with many wonderful surprises." We signed it, "Love, Jody and John Dreyer." People went nuts because most didn't even know we were dating. We had been pals for so long, they thought we would remain "eternal sweethearts." Our marriage uniting me as Happy–Mickey–Mary Poppins to John Dreyer, my Eeyore–Donald Duck–Jiminy Cricket husband, makes for a complicated and magical relationship.

The Tomorrowland opening, sealed with a
kiss for my Disney sweetheart.

ETERNAL SWEETHEARTS

Are Mickey and Minnie married? During my tenure as a Disney ambassador, the only question asked more often was, "Is Goofy a dog or a man?" (He's a man-dog. Seriously. You just have to deal with it.) And the answer to the question on Mickey and Minnie's relationship status is that they are still going steady.

Mickey and Minnie were introduced to the world in the same movie on the same date. They share a November 18 birthday. Now, there was a time around a milestone birthday that Disney considered Mickey and Minnie Mouse matrimony. Think of the great promotional opportunities to mark the occasion: Mickey and Minnie diamond ring sponsors, a worldwide honeymoon tour of every theme park, weddings in our theme parks inspired by our favorite couple. I remember heated meetings over this issue of mouse marriage. And I mean heated.

In this case, proponents and opponents weren't aligning in the usual camps, and there was no middle ground. Everyone had an entrenched position. I took my place among the purists. Why would we want Mickey and Minnie to marry? *Why would we do this?* I couldn't let it go and eventually developed a list of questions for all of us to answer. Where would the couple live? (Mickey and Minnie already had their own homes in Toon Town.) What if this commitment proved a marketing failure or created a public uproar? We couldn't exactly have their relationship end. And, more uncomfortably, since people would go there (I promise you they would), what about romance and reproduction? Did we really want to subject Minnie and Mickey to speculation about their romantic relationship? Would there be children? How many? The possibilities were too incredible to consider.

I cannot claim credit for much of what I worked on at Disney, but I will proudly take credit for advocating—loudly—that Mickey and Minnie would remain forever and always "eternal sweethearts." Why couldn't there be some mystery surrounding their love affair? Why couldn't we accept a loving couple who might never marry? My fellow purists and I embraced the tag "eternal sweethearts," and together we championed that alternative to marital bliss. Because of my very vocal defense of their right to everlasting courtship, I was given a tag in return. Forever after, I was known as "Pollyanna." I can live with that.

CHAPTER 6

CASTLE GUESTS
Choose to Serve

L eave it to a Disney candelabra to speak the truth that we find our purpose in living for something greater than ourselves. Lumière knew too well the sorry life of a servant who's not serving. We're just "not whole without a soul to wait upon." Our stories miss the point altogether if we think the Story (capital *s*) begins and ends with us. Certainly Disney found its purpose and the secret of its success in providing excellent service to customers, visitors, and tourists. But because words have power to shape our attitudes and actions, we never used those terms—customer, visitors, and tourists—to describe Disney's target audience. Our customers were our *guests*: invited, wanted, and welcome.

Setting the Table:
The Dish on Disney's Approach to Service

Given Disney's reputation for providing legendary service and hospitality, you might think Disney got it right all the time.

Not so. Occasionally we hosted a flop. Before the opening of Tokyo Disneyland in 1983, the food and beverage team consulted "cultural sensitivity experts" who advised Disney to open park restaurants with foods familiar to the Japanese in order to make them feel at home. Rice and fish were on most menus. Chopsticks were standard. Ironically, it turned out that our Japanese guests wanted the *ultimate American experience*. In their minds, that meant hot dogs, fries, and sodas with straws. Shortly after opening, Disney regrouped and revamped many of its Tokyo Disneyland food service locations. The revised menus included more stereo-typically American foods to offer what the guests wanted. So much for cultural sensitivity experts.

I worked on the grand opening team for Disney's next foray into the international theme park business, Euro Disney Resort (now Disneyland Paris). The food and beverage team thought we'd nailed it this time. Operating on the premise that Europeans were like the Japanese, park planners designed restaurants with a typically American flavor. Surely the French would love America's favorite, french fries. Right? Alas, when the park opened, the restaurants went begging for customers. Our French guests were leaving the park for meals and then returning for the rides. Park operators surveyed the guests on their way out to lunch to determine what we'd missed. American fast food? That wasn't the dining experience the French were after. They wanted leisurely dining with European foods and, of course . . . *wine*!

The Japanese and French guests taught Disney many lessons. The most important of those was that in the practice of service and hospitality, it's not the Golden Rule that directs activity, it's the Platinum Rule—not so much doing unto others as you would have done unto *you*, but instead doing unto others as they want done unto *themselves*. You give the guests what they want. Against this backdrop, I learned that "service and hospitality" is indeed an art, and one that, practiced to proficiency, creates a beautiful picture of satisfied guests around a table. (Many tables!) The unfortunate alternative is a picture of empty tables and guests heading to the nearest exit.

A Perfect Pairing

You will notice that I always pair *service and hospitality* as one term. I don't believe service and hospitality are interchangeable, or that you should have one without the other. Happy, satisfied guests require both. Not convinced? Have you ever been assisted by someone as nice as could be but without the know-how to get the job done? On the other hand, you may have been served by someone more than competent, but the experience left you feeling like road kill, as though you'd been run over (and back again), and you have the tire marks to prove it.

Service implies providing a benefit before, during, and after interactions. And *good* service suggests leaving guests *fully* satisfied with their experience. But service is a transactional experience, a fair exchange between parties. *Transformational* guest experiences require something more. They require hospitality. If service is getting it done, then hospitality is loving on people in the process.

In the New Testament, the Bible refers to hospitality with the Greek word *philoxenos* (pronounced *feel-o-zee-nos*, according to my dictionary). It combines the idea of offering brotherly love (*philo*) to a stranger or alien (*xenos*). In Greek the word *hospitality* takes on an intentional meaning that stretches our more conventional understanding of opening our homes and hearts to family, friends, and neighbors. It expresses the idea of befriending and loving the stranger. Wouldn't it be great if every interaction started with the attitude of loving a stranger? This mentality takes what could be a transactional interaction and makes it relational. Hospitality is not an equal exchange. ("We hosted last month. It's their turn.") It's more like an unconditional offering of kindness and genuine affection with no expectation of reciprocity.

Service and hospitality is the alchemy of ability and aptitude that makes for unforgettable guest experiences, both personally and professionally. My still-developing skill in the area comes from being (all bragging aside) a great waitress, spending years in Guest Relations at Walt Disney World, coming from a down-home Midwest upbringing, living in the politely hospitable South, and participating in the *In Search of Excellence* training videos—just part of the curriculum offered to me in the school of life.

No matter the business or even philanthropic pursuit, the importance of this idea can't be overstated. Good service and hospitality generates results and makes us feel oh-so-good. Its opposite—the failure to offer service and hospitality—sincerely and consistently erodes loyalty. As my merchandise bosses used to say, "If our guests go away, you do too." Thankfully our guests come and they return. Around the world, Disney welcomes more than 140 million guests every year. A Disney theme park hosts six of every ten US theme park visitors.[1] In the US parks alone, Disney guests gobble up an estimated 1.6 million turkey legs and 75 million soda pops every year. Many of these loyal, enthusiastic guests are our biggest fans and best advocates. You can meet them on Twitter and Instagram if you search #Disneylove, #Disneyfan,

#Disneygeek, #Disnoid. And yes, some fans show their love with the hashtag #Disneyturkeyleg.

Practiced, Not Perfect

Whether they walk through the door of your home, your retail location, or your web portal, you serve guests, too. And instant surveys that measure service quality in business—not to mention Instagram, which displays impossibly beautiful models of hospitality to imitate on the home front—can paralyze us. Why does it so often feel overwhelming to open our home to guests? Maybe because we think everything has to be "just so" to offer an invitation. Let me remind you (and me): don't fall victim to the "perfection trap." Rest assured the best experiences are usually those that are warm, inviting, heartfelt, and often spontaneous. This is about entering into a relationship, not about displaying perfection. As my dad used to say, "Perfection is the enemy of good." Or put another way, "Better something done imperfectly than nothing done perfectly." All boiled down, southerners have it right. It's living the spirit of, "C'mon over, y'all."

The fact is, service and hospitality is never fully mastered, never perfect. It's practiced. And its practitioners are people, not machines. Here's what I observed when I worked in Guest Relations at Walt Disney World. Among the hundreds of guest comments we would get each day, more than 75 percent of them, both good and bad, were not about the attractions, food, or merchandise, but about Disney cast members, about the folks guests interact with at every point of their visit. The vast majority wanted to tell a story about how a cast member made their visit magical with a smile, a gesture, or some extra attention to detail.

Service and Hospitality (Two-Finger) Pointers

* *Use two-finger pointing.* I will always remember my first day of Guest Relations training. We started with the "two-finger point." It was one of those life lessons with near-universal application, and it was simple: *never, ever* point with one finger. (Any of them.) Always direct guests with two fingers, and avoid pointing at someone or pointing in the air. The one-finger point can be rude, intimidating, and a signal of superiority.

* *Communicate eye-to-eye.* Whenever possible, engage in eye-level conversations. For instance, when I worked at Disney World, I would routinely bend down (kneeling would have dusted up my white knee socks) when a child asked me a question.

* *Ask the guest's name.* Of course, our name tags were an encouragement for guests to connect with cast members on a first-name basis, but I liked to know, in return, the name of the person I was talking to. There's nothing like introducing yourself and making the acquaintance of a new friend and using (not *overusing*) that person's name in conversation. If you need to, feel free to ask the person again how to pronounce their name correctly, or how to spell it if you're more of a visual learner. Remembering someone's name is a simple but significant gesture of hospitality. As the friend-winning, people-influencing Dale Carnegie said, "A person's name is to him or her the sweetest and most important sound in any language." So go ahead and speak their language.

> ✳ *Engage in intentional, not random acts of kindness.* There are no **random** acts of kindness. Acts of kindness are intentional and relational. I think "random acts" is a convenient way either to shirk our responsibility to serve or to swoop in, perform a token act, and split. No relationship needed. Just hit-and-run kindness. That doesn't mean I don't love the spontaneous generosity of paying someone's fast-food bill or making an anonymous donation, or holding a door for someone. But I consider those random acts of courtesy or generosity, and they are not the same as practiced and intentional service and hospitality.

Now, How?

Since I can't resist turning everything into a Mickey Mouse face, I describe the practice of service and hospitality with three intersecting circles. Two large ears and a big smiling face, together explaining the *who*, the *how*, and the *wow*!

The Who

We have to start here because the only way to deliver top-notch service and hospitality is to know what makes your guests happy. Walt was famous for knowing and understanding guests. He didn't attend classes on the subject or even use terms we use today, like *customer-focused*, *customer-centric*, or *customer experience*. But what he *was* fanatical about was putting the guest first. I love this often-quoted Walt mantra: "Give the public everything you can give them, keep the park as clean as you can keep it, and keep it friendly." Walt Disney biographer Bob Thomas writes, "During his visits to Disneyland, Walt was always plussing, looking for ways to improve the appearance of Disneyland and provide more pleasure for the customers."[2] The Disney Press publication *Be Our Guest* shared Walt's preferred method of customer research:

> When it was suggested that an administration building be erected for the management at Disneyland, Walt was vehemently opposed. "I don't want you guys sitting behind desks," he said. "I want you out in the park, watching what people are doing and finding out how you can make the place more enjoyable for them." And, when Walt learned that his staff had been leaving the property to eat lunch, he steamed. "Stand in line with the people . . . don't go off the lot to eat like you guys have been doing. You eat at the park and listen to the people!"[3]

The lesson of ear number one: Do your homework. Spend time listening to your customers—from the minute you open your doors to the time you close them—and make adjustments based on what they tell you. Walt would have loved that Disney later called this study "guestology." The examples of our opening experiences at Tokyo Disney Resort and Disneyland Paris reveal just how important it is to know the expectations of guests and how misleading, and potentially disastrous, assumptions can be.

All guests are VIPs. Walt wasn't only fanatical about putting guests first, he was obsessed with the idea that every guest was a VIP. Early Walt Disney World training manuals expressed it this way:

EVERY GUEST on our entire 42 square miles of property is a VIP whether they are visiting the Magic Kingdom for a day or vacationing in our resort-hotels for a week or more. . . . Remember that 99% of our guests are great people with everything going their way and having the time of their life. They are the easy ones to serve. Your real challenge will be that tiny 1% . . . the guests who are hot, tired, hungry, confused, frustrated and perhaps missing their luggage, ticket books or cameras. Or perhaps all of the above. They may not be very understanding and it may be up to you to turn their day around into the positive kind they came here to experience.

In our home, we recognize guests as VIPs with a note on an entryway chalkboard to welcome them, or, a plate that says "You are special," which we reserve just for visitors. At Disney properties around the world, every guest is a VIP—a Very *Individual* Person with a unique story and a one-of-a-kind personality. Ours is the opportunity to discover what makes every VIP special.

The How

Mickey's second ear and a key ingredient to cooking up over-the-top-notch hospitable service is knowing *how*. This is as easy as remembering your p's and q's—your *p*ractices in offering *q*uality service and down-home hospitality:

Be prepared. Delivering on a service and hospitality promise requires a practiced plan. (We've already dispensed with the idea of a perfect plan. It's a myth. Moreover, "perfect" is personal and depends on the guest.) Even so, you can define what *excellent* service looks like and how to get there. Know the plan and know your stuff. Be an expert in the area of your service and curious enough to continue learning so that when asked you can share meaningful information about the dish you are serving, the cause you represent, or the product you hope to sell.

Be a pro—efficient and effective. My favorite baseball players are the pitchers who come in at the end of the game, the closers. They are brought in to end the game and protect the win. Think of yourself as the hospitality service closer. How do you win the game in a timely and successful way? Peter Drucker, the legendary management consultant, said, "Efficiency is doing things right; effectiveness is doing the right things."[4] Service, done right and on time, is unbeatable.

Be personable. This should be second nature, or at the very least, just what your mama told you: "Mind your manners." Keep courtesy words like *please*, *thank you*, and *you're welcome* at the ready. Words matter. And so does your tone of voice. Bear that in mind when (yet another) guest approaches and asks, "What time is the three o'clock parade?" Because you know what? That guest may know full well the parade starts at 3:00 p.m., but his real question is, "Do we have time to get my cranky toddler an ice cream cone without missing the parade?" Or maybe the guest is trying to say, "I am here with my mom. She's not well but she wants to see the parade one last time to make her trip complete. Will the parade start on time?" Every VIP has a story—and not all of them are magical. Like the familiar quote repeated by recording artist TobyMac, "Be kind for everyone you meet is fighting a battle you know nothing about."

Be positive. One of my favorite exercises that I routinely practiced with tour guide trainees was to try answering every question without ever using the word *no*. So even if "no" was the correct answer to a particular question such as, say, "Can I get a beer somewhere here in the Magic Kingdom?" we might say, "Dinner guests at our Beauty and the Beast themed restaurant may order beer or a glass of wine." Or, "Sir, I can direct you to a great selection of coffees, tea, and soft drinks." (Which is just a more positive way of saying, "No liquid courage for you, sir. You've got to take on Splash Mountain fueled only with a soda pop.") This is fun to try with your family. Pick a no-no day. Challenge each other to go an entire day without saying the word *no*. It's no easy . . . oops. I mean, it's not. . . . Trust me. It's harder than it sounds.

Be proactive. We can remove the "nos" from our responses and eliminate negatives of all kinds by being proactive. Just step out, lend a hand, ask a question, and start the conversation. You won't be sorry. I like to call this being "assertively friendly," not fake or aggressive, but approachable and warm. When guests would arrive at the Magic Kingdom as the park opened, we'd station cast members to welcome and assist them. They would point out the places to find strollers or breakfast, or ask if a guest needed any help in getting to a high priority attraction. Later in the day when the temperatures would soar and patience would plummet, we'd contribute to "PCC"—Parade Crowd Control. This wasn't a show of force to restrain crabby kids, but our opportunity to engage them (or their overwrought parents). We'd suggest a pin trade or ask about the best ride of the day. Sometimes we'd pull them out of the crowd and dance.

So that covers the p's, the practices, that together make up ear number two. So far, we have the *who* and the *how*, but there's also something else—that hard-to-define, harder-to-duplicate, pixie-dust Disney difference. It's the third circle in the Mickey face, the one with the smile. I call it the *wow*!

Words Matter

I like to paraphrase Luke 6:45, "Out of the heart, the mouth speaks." My experience tells me the converse is also true: the heart responds to what the mouth says. I discovered that Disney vocabulary not only set a tone but it shaped a service and entertainment mind-set. Using Disney words like "the show, onstage, offstage, good show, bad show, hosts, and guests" transformed our view of our jobs, or roles, and the folks we served. The pamphlet I referred to earlier called *"Welcome to the Show"* defined our visitors this way: "They are our 'guests,' rather than just to be entertained. We must treat them with our very best personal guest reception." And in our role as "hosts," it said, "We've invited people to come and enjoy our special way of creating happiness. So, wherever you work, you are . . . in fact . . . a host." Speaking those words allows Disney cast members everywhere to embody them.

The Wow

Do you know that feeling when you think the show has ended, and suddenly there's more? Your expectations are exceeded with one more fabulous burst of light in the sky or another ovation-deserving number? These are the moments cast members delight in delivering.

These magical moments can happen when we pay attention to detail, looking for signature ways to make a difference and knowing that these usually involve noticing details that matter. I am reminded of the service surprise I received as a hotel guest at a local resort. When I'd lost something and looked under the bed with hope of finding it, I noticed a card placed there that read, "Yes, we clean under here, too." When I checked in, they didn't tell me about this. It wasn't in the resort literature, but it was that attention to detail that made me feel good about my choice to stay there.

Other ways to *wow* are as easy as making ordinary, daily encounters memorable. It's a matter of listening and looking for opportunities to offer great service and over-the-top hospitality. If you see a negative situation setting up, enter the situation to stop or slow the snowball's momentum. We called these "service saves." If we noticed a child drop an ice cream cone or let go of their balloon, no problem. We replaced it. And if someone got off Space Mountain to discover their Mickey Mouse ears had fallen into a black hole, we walked them over to the nearest store and got others. (Last I knew, Disney World collected about eighteen thousand hats a year in the lost and found.) Out of dark situations come some of the best service saves, because rays of sunshine are always more noticeable through the clouds.

I have dozens of extraordinary service and hospitality examples I could share, because Disney empowers cast members to make magic. Sometimes it was just an extra pin that we could award, or a simple and spontaneous kindness—whatever it took to make a magical moment. I'm so grateful for that early practice, because in our typically hurried days, it doesn't always come naturally to focus on the people around us. But I am telling you, when you can be the catalyst to a magical moment, there is no better feeling.

These days when Disney instructs on *wow* experiences, they encourage cast members to "own the moment." Theme park managers have estimated there are over eleven billion ways a guest can interact with the Disney promise in just the Orlando Walt Disney World Resort alone.[5] These are the total possible interactions guests can have with attractions, food, products, entertainment, characters, transportation, or any other Disney World element. *Eleven billion!* You can't script the right way to handle billions of possible interactions, but you can equip and empower people to seize the moments to surprise and amaze your guests—to *choose* to go the extra mile for exceptional service and hospitality. Chick-Fil-A calls this practice "second mile service." It's more than operating a clean restaurant and serving good food. That's expected. Second mile service is when employee brings food to your table or stops by to see if you would like a drink refill. It's when employees stage an impromptu party to celebrate the end of a guest's chemo treatments. Going the first mile can be obligatory, but going the second mile—cheerfully and voluntarily—is service supersized.

Hospitality and service are choices, not accidents. Every day, putting the welfare of others before your own and going the extra mile on their behalf is a "you-before-me" mind-set. It can be taught and talked about in volumes of books and blogs, but ultimately it's a choice. And that choice can become a mission and a passion and, ultimately, what defines you.

Hospitable service is optional. We are reminded of this every time we have an exceptionally good service experience. Likewise, you recognize the extra effort when you've been invited to someone's home and you've been made to feel that your visit was a gift—to the *host*. What if the gift isn't in the *giving* of service and hospitality but in *receiving* the guest? What if the guest on whom you bestow exceptional service and hospitality, in your business or home, has something special for you?

When we open our doors and our hearts to those we meet—

wherever we find them—and extend to them authentic and grace-filled hospitality we may receive more than we give. Let the candlestick Lumière shed a little light on the subject. In the film, the castle door opens to Belle's father, a lost and shaken Maurice. Paying no heed to Cogsworth's admonishment, the candlestick invites Maurice to enter and warm himself by the fire—just a simple act of kindness to a stranger. But with that invitation to an unexpected castle guest, Lumière clears a path for the events that would set him free. (And lead him to a future with a winsome feather-duster-turned-French-maid named Babette—who, by the way, was played by our niece in Disney's traveling stage production of *Beauty and the Beast*. Oo la la, Erin!)

Niece Erin as Babette in Disney's *Beauty and the Beast* traveling show.

PUT A SMILE IN YOUR VOICE

Disney believes that exceptional guest service experiences begin before guests even step foot on theme park property. Many guest experiences begin on the phone. In my early days of guest service training, each of us assigned in the park would also take a turn "working in the forty-five hundred." That stood for the number guests dialed when they were requesting park information or brochures. Good ol' (407) 824–4500. (Remember, there was no internet then. Disney information was gathered with a phone call.)

Disney Guest Service representatives rotated through park assignments and had at least one shift in the 4500. The benefit was twofold: Disney figured rightly that cast members with regular park experience would be more knowledgeable about the park's operations. And Disney also believed that the way prospective guests were treated on the phone could be the difference between booking a great vacation or not. We were reminded that we could be the first Disney cast member someone would encounter, and we were encouraged to answer the phone with a "smile in our voice." You might think that was just a mindgame. Actually, the reason to smile as you answer the phone is physiological. Smiling changes the position of the soft palate in your mouth and makes the sound waves more fluid, so your voice sounds more like singing. (Try it.) This answers the age-old question: If you smile in the 4500 and no one is there to see it, does it still make a sweeter sound?

CHAPTER 7

GO TEAM!

All Together Now

Heigh-ho, heigh-ho, when off to work I went, I was daily reminded of how much The Walt Disney Company values teamwork. In US headquarter locations, and in Hong Kong and Paris, cast members report to buildings called "Team Disney." I worked for a long time at the Team Disney Burbank building, designed by famed architect Michael Graves. Its distinctive design features nineteen-foot-tall dwarfs (in a classic oxymoron) who appear to be supporting the building's pediment. In tribute to Disney's first feature film megahit, the building design also celebrates teams with its visual statement that many hands can make light work of even the heaviest lifting. One of my offices looked out on a popular location for nesting birds, right under Sleepy's armpit.

Even in the armpit of a classic Disney character, my job there as the senior vice president of synergy was tailor-made for me. I *love* teams! I love the spirit, the camaraderie, and the truth that teams can do together what individuals can't accomplish alone. We might not have it all together, but together we have it all.

The Sound of Synergy

Walt's groundbreaking feature film, *Fantasia*, premiered in November 1940. It was the creative masterpiece that married Disney animation to classical music. Mickey, as the Sorcerer's Apprentice, was introduced in the third sequence. The unusual name of Mickey's master? It's Yen Sid, and it's of no particular culture or ethnicity. The name is "Disney" spelled backward. More importantly, *Fantasia* demonstrated (once again) Walt's unceasing drive for excellence. Not satisfied with an audio experience that would detract from the visual experience of the film, Walt and his teams created the forerunner to surround sound. The technology was called "Fantasound." From hundreds of systems designed on paper (and then scrapped), and ten built for testing, eventually one system was perfected and installed in only fourteen cinemas across the nation. Fantasound replaced the audio technology of the era (a single speaker behind the movie screen) with the world's first stereophonic sound reproduction system.[5] Oh, the sweet sounds of synergy.

All Together Now

At Disney this teamwork was often called *synergy*. As of this writing, it could be called integration, synchronization, or even collaboration. Whatever the name, the concept is the same: individual parts blending in harmony, creating something more magical together than any could create individually. My love of sports owes largely to this truth about teams. Synergistic teams share three important elements: skilled coaching, talented and well-equipped players, and a game plan. We've already talked about leadership and the importance of knowing who's in charge—that person appointed to set the game plan, call the shots, and perhaps most important, get out of the way when it's time to let the players play. Position coaches, strength and conditioning coaches, and assistant coaches all play roles in leading a team to greatness. You also need well-trained, properly equipped players of all sorts—like your diverse cast of characters. Depending on the sport, there are defenders, scorers, position players, substitutes, and starters, all of whom are imperative for teams that go the distance. (And we shouldn't forget the trainers, groundskeepers, equipment managers, and those behind the field of play who contribute to the win.) Teams can be big or small. I think of families as teams. Businesses can form teams that break down into smaller teams, so can churches and clubs. And if achieving a common goal matters to the group—whatever the size—synergy is the fuel that invigorates their collaboration. Finally, but mission critical to any great team, is the game plan. Walt knew this. He summarized it with these words: "Of all the things I've done, the most vital is coordinating those who work with me and aiming their efforts at a certain goal."[1]

Teams need a game plan the way orchestras need a song. Each instrument can be perfectly tuned with a virtuoso in command, but if musicians set their own tempo to dissimilar tunes of their choosing, nothing about the result is harmonic. "Singing from the same song sheet" is not a quaint old idiom, it's a must for orchestras as well as teams. What's the common goal? The rallying cry? What does success look like today, tomorrow, and in the future?

Disney created lots of plans, and even plans for making plans. There were quarterly plans, yearly plans, and five-and ten-year plans. Depending on the area, some departments even relied on daily or hourly work plans, all critical to getting everyone on the same page and working collaboratively. These departmental plans rolled up to divisional plans and ultimately the company game plan, which detailed both short-term and long-term goals and priorities. You knew your individual goals and priorities, and you also knew the priorities of cast members around you and of the larger team.

Within each division (Studios, Theme Parks, Consumer Products, Television, ESPN, and others) there were individuals tasked with keeping the information flowing (collectively, *hundreds* of Synergy Superstars). I need a standing ovation here for my Synergy brothers and sisters—you are the best of the best! These consummate team players tweaked and trimmed plans as situations changed, but we never operated without one. And as Coach Wooden is known for saying, "Failing to prepare is preparing to fail."

To Be Together Is to Be Together

To understand your position and others' is crucial to synergy and successful teamwork. In my experience, the only way for this understanding to take place is to be in relationship. I learned this during my year as Disney World's ambassador, and it was a lesson I delighted in. To be together is to be together. Or, to be together *requires* you to be together. It takes time, interaction, and focus to do that.

The 1971 opening year of Walt Disney World with the Carbiener kids at Magic Kingdom.

That first tour with Leo inspired my dreams to wear the tour guide tartan myself one day.

Sharing the thrill of the Ambassador announcement moment with Mom and Dad.

The Service Award Ceremony was a formal affair in celebration of Walt Disney World's birthday.

What a unique privilege to take the characters to visit
precious children in hospitals around the world.

The grand opening of the Living Seas Pavilion at Epcot Center.

All aglow after lighting the Rockefeller Center
Christmas tree with a host of Disney characters.

Ambassador training was serious and seriously fun with
pals Hiroko Saito (Tokyo Disneyland Ambassador 1986, left)
and Barb Warren (Disneyland Ambassador 1986, right).

All hands on deck allowed smooth sailing for the Disney Cruise Line inaugural voyage.

John Dreyer and I about to boat to the future site of Hong Kong Disneyland for the groundbreaking announcement.

Euro Disneyland site prior to the 1992 opening when hard hats replaced mouse ears.

Photo courtesy of Sylvie Laffarge, my first French friend and magnifique team member.

Parade can-can dancer, one of the best jobs ever!

Long days made for lasting memories of the Euro Disney Grand Opening Team. Pictured here with two of my hard-working teammates: Kim Piercy and Rick Allen.

Roy E. Disney (Walt's nephew) was a wealth of firsthand Disney history.

Janis and I with Mickey and Minnie Mouse and the Li**mouse**ine.

CEO Michael surprised me with a birthday cake during a show taping, orchestrated by synergy guru Jonathan (Garson) and fairy godmother Virgie.

What a team! Working the Tokyo Disney Seas Grand
Opening was one of many events captained by
Patrick Alo, Lady Di Connors, and Barry Jacobson.
Photo courtesy of Marsha Reed, also of event extravaganza fame.

Jody with Mom and Dad at the entrance of Tokyo Disneyland.

My turn to take Sister Fifi
and Baby Mike on a tour.
Photo courtesy of top tour guide
and friend, Joel Curran.

Big Brother Chip's frosted castle
was enjoyed by guests for Disney
World's twenty-fifth anniversary
and by his children, Bud and Katie.

Carbiener Farm cornfield at dawn.
Photo courtesy of John Dreyer.

The more we know each other and our mutual strengths and weaknesses, and understand each other's positions, the more we can work seamlessly and in harmony. Stacy has a friend who has been a soprano in the Cleveland Orchestra Chorus. She said that once you master the notes for your section, singing alongside a vocalist in a different section (a soprano singing next to a tenor, for example) makes your contribution stronger. Confident in your role, when you tune your efforts to those around you, the result is even more harmonious. We can all be different while still singing together—and from the same song sheet. As Jen Hatmaker says, "We needn't mistake unity with uniformity; we can have the first without the second."[2]

Disney invested time and resources to make sure the various and distinct business units understood and appreciated one another. Perhaps the best example was a program called Disney Dimensions. Designed for senior executives from across the company and around the globe, participants were personally invited by Michael (Eisner), then CEO and Chairman of the Board, to join in the synergy-building exercise. Michael prized teamwork. The invitation, in part, read like this:

> Disney Dimensions presents the big picture of our Company. Even though our businesses are run in an entrepreneurial fashion, we know that synergy is one of the keys to even greater success. Disney Dimensions is the ultimate synergy program in that it brings together 20 executives from across the entire Company, representing our domestic, regional and international offices for an intense, nine-day examination of every facet of our organization. The program encourages candid conversations with top executives and

reinforces what it is we all are here to do, which is to provide quality entertainment to our audiences and to perpetuate the magic that is associated with the Disney name.

I was privy to the invitation because part of my job as the head of synergy included managing these immersion experiences. Being invited was an honor, and surviving the nine days was a badge of pride! The intensity and adventure of the itinerary led to its internal nickname: Disney Dimension Boot Camp. It was a nine-day Disney march starting at Team Disney Burbank and ending at Team Disney Orlando, with stops in Anaheim, Bristol, Connecticut, and New York City in between. Our days began before sunrise and ended well into the night. The goal was to "dip" these Disney executives in all of our business unit activities so they could experience as much of the Disney magic and its making as possible.

Only limited access to cell phones, computers, and offices was allowed, so that participants could stay laser focused on the program. In his book *Work in Progress*, Michael (Eisner) described the experience this way:

> What they [participants] love first is hating us for making them participate. But after a few days, they embrace the Outward Bound–style camaraderie that grows out of enduring a punishing schedule together. They also appreciate the concentrated education they receive and the relationships they form. When they return to their jobs, and they need help from an executive in another division, they no longer have to call a stranger, but can turn instead to a foxhole companion from Disney Dimensions. The company, and the brand, derive the benefit.[3]

When you talk to former executives about their time at Disney, they will often mention as a highlight the close friendships formed during their time at boot camp (I mean, Dimensions). It was thrilling to lead these programs where I witnessed firsthand the evolution of a group of fiercely independent, successful executives who begin the program each with their own agenda and preconceptions who, by the end of the week, form a team committed to their mutual success—*and* to each other.

A typical day included activities like a helicopter tour of Walt Disney World and a quick stop at each theme park, followed by participating in a finance meeting to examine numbers and priorities. (One year we wrapped up with a screening of *Toy Story*, which would premier thirty days later. So, there were some lighter moments in the program. And a point well made too: *You've got a friend in me*.) Make no mistake, this program was expensive, logistically challenging, and time consuming, but I received a valuable life lesson in the process: to know and understand is to appreciate and value. And this understanding of the wide reach of Disney, the depth of the talent within the company, and the height of our mutual challenges and opportunities added, just as promised, *a whole new dimension* to our collaborative efforts.

Fight, Team, Fight!
(Of Rules, Wrongs, and Rescues)

Not only have I learned that all good teams need a practiced playbook and plan, but they also need to understand a few other essentials. Let's call these the rules, wrongs, and rescues.

The Rules

The first place most of us learn the rules of the game is at home in our families. I can't think of a better place to learn that the game only works with established boundaries around the field of play and limits to our behaviors. It was these family rules that fostered teamwork in the Carbiener family. We had big kids and little ones, girls and boys, and mostly everyone got along except for the usual day-to-day eruptions: "She borrowed my clothes and didn't give them back!" "He's picking on me!" "Do I have to take the little kids with me?" You know, the stuff that can send parents' heads flying off their bodies. Because my mom and dad could tolerate very little of this, we operated under their three-step plan for acceptable behavior: name it; claim it; and make it better. Step one—name it—was a mandate to call it as we see it or say, "Here's what's happening, and it's unacceptable." This was followed by step two—claim it: If you know what's good for you, you'll own up to it. (Which is also the origin of the "no excuses" mandate, also very big in my family.) It was okay to misbehave or to make mistakes, but when you were called out, you'd better man up. And last (typically the hardest of the three-step plan), Make it better—or make it right. For the most part, this was simply an apology in the form of a written note, and very often penned in crayon during the ages when they were the tool of choice.

Speaking of family and family rules, one of the best codes of conduct I learned from my baby brother. Mike was the captain of his high school golf team. Fair warning—don't ever let him persuade you to wager on a casual round of golf. I've learned my lesson. Mike will take your money and make it look all too easy, which can make people really cranky. Crankiness aside, what I do love about the game is that the rules of golf originated out of courtesy for fellow players and a concern for fairness. How great is that?

There are no zebra-striped refs in golf. This is a gentleman's (and lady's) game. Every player is expected to be honest, even in the face of a bad lie. And then there's one of my favorite golf practices—the "mulligan." It's not an official USGA rule, but a universally accepted one among amateurs of all skill levels, and the best example of allowing someone a second chance. Plain and simple, it's a "do-over." Couldn't we all use a mulligan every once in a while?

Life Is a Highway

One of the most fun collaborations I've been a part of happened as a result of our Dimensions program. Disney built a country music label named Lyric Street Records. The founder and head of the label, Randy (Goodman), was a participant in the program. Anyone who knows Randy would agree he's a great leader personifying character and team spirit. During our travels, Randy told me about a new group Lyric Street had signed. He was eager to have the rest of the company hear them and see if there were any opportunities to give the group greater exposure. You've probably heard of the group—Rascal Flatts. (You know, that multi-platinum trio and six-time Country Music Association Vocal Group of the year winner? Yeah, them.) We were able to arrange "meet and greets" and mini concerts. Eventually the group was introduced to Pixar's John Lasseter, a ginormous country music fan. Rascal Flatts's cover of *Life Is a Highway* became a Billboard hit after its release on the soundtrack of the 2006 Disney/Pixar animated movie *Cars*. That was textbook synergy. Nothing was forced. It was the organic outcome of strategic-minded team players working together for the common good.

The Wrongs

We needn't belabor this, but there are a few behaviors that can take the air out of teamwork and synergy faster than a nine iron to the stomach. So it's important to establish some general rules. First, *no whining*—that irritating "art" of complaining or blaming so persistently that your misery ends up being shared by everyone in your vicinity. I understand sharing each other's burdens. I encourage that. But enough already. Recognize the difference between registering a complaint and broadcasting one. Keep the whining to a minimum. Second, *no backstabbing.* If you have anything to say, get it out. Be up front and insist on open and honest communication. What might be hard to hear face-to-face can be shattering when you hear it on the street. Shut down that kind of talk. Here's an expression you can use to quiet a backstabber: "I am sorry to hear you say that. She always has such nice things to say about you." Finally, consider your teammates like a nature preserve: *no dumping.* We all share the load. Some days your burden is heavier than others. The next day, your load might be lighter. We can take one for the team every so often if generally we all pull our own weight.

Even in a happy place like Disney, we all committed our share of penalties. I discovered, though, that the more we called out the penalties, the less frequently they were committed. It always amazes me what heights folks can reach when you set the bar high. This is true personally and professionally. All teams, families, and organizations need a code of acceptable behavior. And within those boundaries, you want all the teams in the "league" to play hard. In those intense game situations, fouls happen. In the Disney league, there was always competition among business units. Mostly it was healthy and appropriate, but now and again we needed an authority to whistle a stop to rough play and send everyone to the sidelines to cool off.

Perhaps the greatest of these referees at Disney was Sandy (Litvack), the company's general counsel. In his earlier life, he had been a trial lawyer and assistant attorney general in the antitrust division of the Department of Justice. He has even argued a case before the Supreme Court. I think that uniquely qualified him to listen to Disney plaintiffs and defendants alike, hearing all sides of the case with impartiality before pronouncing a verdict. He was a real-life Jiminy Cricket with some wise Owl from Winnie the Pooh mixed in. He was known for saying (and living), "Integrity is the one thing that can't be taken from you. If you lose it, you've given it away."

The Rescues

The flipside to penalty-incurring behaviors are self-sacrificing assists. There is nothing like a good assist, a player coming to the rescue, setting up a teammate to go for the win. Oh, yes, it's pure beauty to behold.

I learned about assists the hard way growing up in a lacrosse-playing family. In high school I was the statistician for my big brother, Chip's, team. More impactfully, my little sister Fifi and I (when we couldn't avoid it) were stand-in practice goalies—until we realized how many shots on goal they took and how much those small rubber balls traveling at high speeds could hurt. The heart of my stat duty was to count ground balls scooped up and assists that led to scoring. Here's what I learned from lacrosse: The person with the most assists usually also had the most goals. And the person winning the most ground balls often had the most assists and goals. Hmm. So if you connect the dots, it would make sense that the hustlers getting a lot of ground balls, who are not afraid to pass the ball (even if they aren't the ultimate scorer), would also score quite often. As Big Bro Chip (best lacrosse coach ever) would say, you have to have the ball . . . to make great passes . . . to make goals . . . to win games.

Disney has its own version of promoting game-winning assists with its theme park program Cross Utilization, Cross-U for short. It is the epitome of jumping in to lend a hand. During peak times in the parks, such as when schools are out but before seasonal cast members are on board, back-of-the-house cast members will take shifts in the parks to help handle the rush. Now, not to worry—it isn't as if an accountant is driving your monorail. All the same, extra hands and feet are a big help in distributing items or working crowd control. Cast members might grumble a bit (without whining) about the extra hours they're asked to work. And these extra duties can put cast members behind in their own job responsibilities, but they generally take one for the team. Not only is Cross-U a great example of pitching in and helping out, but it's also an opportunity to walk in someone else's shoes for a day. I love how the company incorporates this program into park operations. It says to me that in our organization, we take care of each other. Cast members were often reminded that Walt himself encouraged his fellow filmmakers to work as a team to produce an orchestrated effort, and that, at all times, we should treat each other as we might our treasured theme park guests. We'd all be well served to think of our teammates, in whatever setting we meet them, as family. As Lilo explains to Stitch, "*Ohana* means family. *Family* means no one gets left behind." I have your back, and you have mine.

Working some Cross Utilization (Cross-U)
at Big Thunder Mountain Railroad.

Good Sports

It seems only fitting that one of the Disney business units that
would take to synergy from the word *go* would be ESPN. In
1996 when Disney acquired ABC/Cap Cities (a majority-owner
of ESPN), one of the first calls we received was from George
(Bodenheimer), former head of ESPN. He knew that there could
be great potential in collaborating with Disney's varied business
units, and also great opportunity to learn from folks in ventures
less familiar to them. He was one of the first attendees of Disney

Dimensions from the newly acquired ABC/ESPN, and he was hardwired for hustle and team play. So much so, that he was one of the first to create a designated synergy group within his division. In mere months, they were "synergizing" with Disney business units from the theme parks to consumer products. ESPN Zones can be found at Walt Disney World and Disneyland, ESPN merchandise is sold at locations around the world, and annual ESPN events are held at various Disney locations. Maybe George understood the potential upside from years of working in and around teams, or maybe he was just a natural leader and team player. All I know is that it worked.

Win, Team, Win!

For much of my Disney career, I was tasked with the job of stoking the fires of company synergy. While it's hard to pick my favorite job during my thirty years at Disney, Corporate Synergy had to be high on my list. Working with so many areas of the company and interacting with talented, committed, passionate characters was the best part. The clearest way to explain the job is to say I was the traffic controller in a busy company. From my vantage point, I prevented collisions and looked for opportunities for people to work together for the corporate good, which generally meant sharing best practices, celebrating successes, and, most important, facilitating the flow of information among business units around the world. What a view I had. For as much as I learned about the inner workings of Disney, what I learned about creating high-functioning, synergistic teams is simple. But simple isn't always easy. Here are three simple truths:

✳ **Number One: Informed teams are transformed teams.** Communicate. Communicate. Communicate. No matter the sport, every successful team knows you have to talk—coaches to players, players to each other, support folks to coaches and players, and then back again. It is an information circle that must keep spinning with a constant feeding of new information. Because the more you know, the more teams grow. And this is especially true for dynamic and collaborative groups. Information is the fuel that keeps synergy burning bright.

✳ **Number Two: Bend, don't break.** Flexibility is the capacity to adapt and change throughout the game. Accept adjustments as part of the plan. As you assess the situation and recognize your strengths and weaknesses and the relative effectiveness of the plan, don't be reluctant to make a midcourse correction. Pixar's cofounder, Ed Catmull, encouraged his teams to "fail fast." Move aggressively toward the goal and accept redirects as an integral, and even welcome, part of progress.

✳ **Number Three: Celebrate the *Aha!* moments.** When teams play their best, resulting in wins for the team and personal bests for the players, take the time to recognize the achievement and celebrate. Don't limit the celebration to *W*'s on the scoreboard. When someone takes one for the team or gives a little something extra so someone else gets a win, put them on your shoulders and take a victory lap. Recognition provides encouragement, and people notice. Members of the team should feel not only a responsibility to do their part, but to bring others along as well. We called these synergy conversions—those *aha!* moments that deserve a cheer.

Strength in Numbers

Have you ever demonstrated the strength-in-numbers exercise? Take one toothpick or twig and see how easy it is to break in two, then put about five together and see if you can crack them in half. What about a bundle of ten? Bet you can't break them. Power, strength, and success are found in coming together, working together, and being together.

Young Life's work in Africa is an example of this. Launched in 2002 in one country, today more than 830,000 kids are being impacted in twenty-four African countries. The Young Life Africa folks have a motto they live by. In Swahili the motto is: *Pamoja, pamoja.* To you and me it means, "Together, together—as one."

Speaking of Africa, my friend Don (Hahn), the producer of *The Lion King*, recently wrote to me on the subject of teamwork in film-making. He had this to say:

> The single thing I try to do is create a safe place for the team. That means a safe workplace to bring up any idea that might help "plus" the film. The idea of "plussing" is something that Walt loved...the thought that a good idea can be made great by pushing it higher and higher into its best possible form.
>
> The other secret is that I try to hire the best possible people that I can find, and then stay out of their way. Nobody needs a helicopter boss hovering over the process. Yes, if you're Walt Disney or Steve Jobs, you are a once-in-a-generation talent who can hover and make great work, but even those two guys hired the best and brightest and let them run with ideas. So to recap: Great people, safe room, plussing it until it's great. There is no good...there is only great.

When Teamwork Makes a Miracle

I can't write about teams without a mention of my favorite Disney sports movie of all time, *Miracle*. The film is based on the true story of the 1980 Winter Olympics gold-medal-winning US hockey team. This underdog team made up of club and college players took on a Goliath competitor, the Soviet Union national team (who were funded and trained like pros though they were called amateurs). The Americans' win in this epic battle inspired announcer Al Michaels's now famous question uttered in the final seconds of the game: "Do you believe in miracles?"

Every point I make in this chapter plays out in this captivating, suspenseful, moving story about a group of individuals who become a history-making team. At its finest, synergy owes its success to a passionate coach with a plan, players applying their skills and work ethic to unselfish team play, and a supporting cast who contribute less evident but indispensable efforts.

But here's a part of the story that didn't get as much press as the historic win. The final player cut from the team was Ralph Cox. He was a record-setting scorer at the University of New Hampshire. He suffered a broken ankle during the sixty-two-game pre-Olympic tour, and he wasn't recovering quickly enough. Coach Herb Brooks cut him from the team the night before they were to travel to Lake Placid. (But not without compassion. Brooks himself had been the last player cut from the 1960 Olympic team.) You'd have thought this competitor would have had only sour grapes about the turn of events. Instead, years later, Cox said this: "I never played hockey for one moment. I played hockey for always. I played hockey because I loved it. . . . I traveled the world with hockey and made friendships that last to this day. I always felt if I went to the Olympics I wouldn't have met my wife and had two terrific kids. . . . I've got no should'ves and could'ves."[4] That's the definition of success in synergy: knowing the team's victory is also your own.

A SYNERGISTIC HAT TRICK

In December 1992, the National Hockey League had just awarded the newest hockey franchise to The Walt Disney Company. On the surface it didn't seem to make a lot of sense (CEO Michael himself had said that professional sports is rarely a good business), but as the story started to unfold, the opportunities for synergy became clear. Disney was hoping to attract guests to Disneyland who would stay longer than a day, but at the time, Anaheim didn't offer much else to hold the attention of visitors. To stimulate tourism, the city had constructed a $110 million sports arena on the "if-come" premise—if you build it, they will come. The problem was, no one did. No professional sports team was especially interested. Enter serendipity—Michael's love of hockey and his boys' involvement in the sport had prompted him (really, it was his oh, so smart wife, Jane) to suggest commissioning a script for a hockey movie. That script became the widely popular Disney movie *The Mighty Ducks*. Just before its release, Michael received a call from the owner of the Los Angeles Kings hockey team to see if Disney might be interested in owning a hockey franchise, bringing a second team to Southern California.

So, let's take stock: Disneyland had motivation to enhance Anaheim's draw; Anaheim had an expensive sports facility to fill; and *The Mighty Ducks* movie could provide lots of cross-promotional opportunities to support a new team. Sounds like a synergistic hat trick. So sixty-nine days after *The Mighty Ducks'* opening, the NHL awarded its expansion franchise to The Walt Disney Company. The new team was named, synergistically, the Mighty Ducks.

John Dreyer and Wild Wing, the
original Mighty Ducks mascot.

This project was a career highlight for John Dreyer, my Eeyore. He is a *huge* hockey fan, and being present at the franchise agreement signing and supervising the publicity around the awarding of the franchise to Disney was an absolute thrill. It was special for both of us, because the deal was announced just weeks after our wedding and during the time of our move to California. One of my first assignments in my new role as head of synergy was to integrate the team. (High fives to Jenny [Price], my partner in all things Angels and Ducks.) We created ticket package promotions, hockey nights at Disneyland, and even a company-wide contest to design the logo and identity package. The winning idea came from the TV animation division, and they celebrated at the Ducks' opening game. It was apparent from the first puck drop in the newly built (Arrowhead) Pond that this was teamwork at its best. (As a postscript, the Mighty Ducks were sold in 2005 and renamed the Anaheim Ducks. The following season they won the Stanley Cup.) Disney's ownership of the team accomplished everything the company had hoped for. It was a win for all parties, even if it didn't continue. Some synergistic relationships last in perpetuity, and others only for a season—or twelve.

CHAPTER 8

WHO KNEW?

It Only Looks Like Magic

On October 25, 1985, at 11:00 a.m. in the Cinderella Castle Forecourt, families of the Walt Disney World Ambassador finalists, past ambassadors, and Magic Kingdom guests, cast members, and media gathered around for a special announcement. The event moderator read a proclamation describing the role and mission of The Walt Disney World Ambassador, a proclamation that has been recited every year since 1971. It began:

> Hear ye! Hear ye! Citizens of all nations, be it known that the Walt Disney World Ambassador will represent Walt Disney World and the millions of happy citizen vacationers....

After reciting the official duties of the ambassador, in a final flourish, the moderator said, "For 1986, the Official Walt Disney World Ambassador to the World is . . . Jody Jean Carbiener." Off went the fireworks. Up went the birds. There were hoots and hollers and dancers and singers.

While less than flattering, this photo captures my shock
at being named Walt Disney World Ambassador.

Aside from the fact that the photo capturing the moment
would have you believe I'd been punched in the stomach, this
was one of the most exciting, life-changing moments of my life.

But first, a little background. The Disney Ambassador Program
started in 1965 at Disneyland. At the time, Walt was managing
the buzz following the 1964 New York World's Fair and Disney's
four attractions there (including It's a Small World), the developing
Project X (aka Walt Disney World), and the upcoming celebration
of Disneyland's tenth anniversary. Even Walt with his boundless
energy couldn't be everywhere as the namesake and embodiment
of Disney magic, so Jack (Lindquist), the spirited and imaginative
head of Disneyland marketing at that time, proposed the concept
of a theme park ambassador. Walt loved the idea.

Disneyland tour guide Julie Reihm (Casaletto) was named

the first ambassador. Julie was referred to as Miss Disneyland Tencennial. Though the program was intended to be a one-year solution to a growing publicity need, it was so successful that it was continued and expanded. For its 1971 opening, Walt Disney World unveiled its own ambassador program, minus the "Miss Walt Disney World" title. The first ambassador, who set the bar high and still serves as a spokesperson today, was Debby Dane (Brown). Today there are ambassadors from each of the parks—Disneyland, Walt Disney World, Tokyo Disney Resort, Disneyland Paris, Hong Kong Disneyland, and Shanghai Disneyland. The ambassadors are a Disney presence around the globe, attending special events, spreading goodwill, hosting dignitaries, and representing their theme park's cast members and characters as the official park spokesperson and host. Walt himself described the early selection criteria, saying the ambassador should be the personification of Disneyland's world-famous spirit of friendliness and happiness.

So back to my punched-in-the-stomach moment. Once the announcement was made and I was presented with my special-issue Mickey ambassadorial pin, I was swept into intensive and extensive training to learn as much as possible about Disney generally, and Walt Disney World specifically. At the start of my term, Walt Disney World had more than ten thousand cast members, many of whom worked in backstage areas with which I wasn't overly familiar. I had only worked in Merchandise, Entertainment, Guest Relations, Seminar Productions, and Marketing at that point in my Disney career. I did have a good start on meeting people and knowing my way around, but wow, I felt ill-equipped to serve as the official spokesperson for areas I knew nothing about. That's when I hit upon this idea: What if I spent the year trying to visit every department at Walt Disney World, meeting as many cast members as possible?

Louise (Gerow), the Walt Disney World Ambassador coordinator, was the perfect person to help me with this. She has a love for all people that is matched only by her love of all things Disney. She had been with the company for decades and knew where to go and whom to call for just about anything you could imagine. Even better, Louise was a blast to be with. And how about this fun fact? She and her husband, Hank, are the only people I've ever met to have actually attended Woodstock. Thank goodness for her spirit, since the ambassadors and Louise spent the year attached at the hip. I shared with her my crazy idea of trying to visit all of the departments, and we were off and running. Sometimes literally. And I didn't just want to show up in a department to say hi, in a hit-and-run goodwill visit. I wanted to go deeper and learn what my fellow cast members did every day. I went to Costuming to don the outfit if there was one, and shadowed cast members, spending time working with them. I wanted to know how my fellow cast members performed their roles and what they loved about their work. (Because like every guest, every cast member has a story.)

There were many highlights to my year as ambassador, among them celebrating Disney World's fifteenth anniversary by giving away magical birthday presents—like keys to cars; touring with our ten-story, Mickey Mouse–shaped, hot-air balloon called *Earforce One*; visiting Michael Jackson at his Neverland Ranch (complete with llamas and mini attractions) to prepare for the opening of his 3-D, sci-fi musical film, *Captain EO*; and guiding former Chief Justice Warren Burger through the park (a personal highlight because he was supernaturally smart in a super, natural way). All of those were out-of-this world, fantastic experiences, but I have to say, meeting the cast in *their worlds* and areas of expertise was the best. I wish I could share about all of the people, places, and passions I encountered in my wandering and discovery, but I'm going to give you some insight into five departments that might surprise you the way they did me.

Key Control: The Keys to the Magic Kingdom

Any kingdom of any significance must have keys, right? Walt Disney World is no exception. During my tenure, I discovered a department charged with securing the kingdom, aptly named Key Control. Located underneath Cinderella Castle, it was about the size of a large garage, but it was an unusual garage to be sure. Along every wall from floor to higher than I could reach were keys, locks, and any gadget you can imagine to keep Disney World safe and secure. Today much of Disney World's security is performed with digital devices and systems, but the area still has the same personality that I recall so clearly. The attitude of the cast members and the camaraderie in Key Control were contagious. These are folks that the typical guest will never see, meet, or even hear about (unless you find yourself locked in the castle), but they were amazing. And they threw the best Christmas potluck party *ever*. Their subterranean world was characterized with kindness and teamwork all around, all the time. Honestly, after I worked with them, I would visit as often as possible just to hang out and get a good old dose of happy. If any cast members had the lock on Disney magic (so to speak) and the key to making work feel like fun, it was my friends in Key Control.

Housekeeping: Spit Spot. I Worked a Lot.

During my ambassador stint, Disney World had more than two thousand rooms on their property, and each and every day those rooms had to be cleaned for our guests. It was a daunting proposition, and my gut said these had to be some of the hardest working folks at Walt Disney World. You know what? My gut was right—*you have no idea!* Let me tell you, if you think you're in good shape, if you think you're a hard worker, and if you think you can make a bed properly, think again. The week I spent in Housekeeping was perhaps the hardest week of work in my life. I will say that I can now make a pretty mean bed, complete with hospital corners. Regrettably, I never mastered forming animals out of the white bath towels.

Housekeeping cast members do some back-breaking work for guests' sweet dreams.

(Some animal shapes were taught to all housekeepers, like a Mickey head—one large towel and two hand towels in circles. Other cast members created their own unique character designs—called "towel-agami"—that they shared with teammates. Some even brought in their own stickers and pipe cleaners to make even more ornate figures.) It was all I could do to keep up with the routine work of preparing a resort room for its next guests. And believe me, they were cutting me plenty of slack. Disney's housekeepers have perfected a creative and efficient process to present guest-ready rooms in quick fashion, and they've managed to add a "wow" along the way.

Pest Control: The SWAT Team

One of my favorite things to do at any Disney theme park around the world is to sit on Main Street and eat popcorn. Did you know the popcorn tastes different depending on which park you are visiting? The popcorn at Disneyland Paris is seasoned with sugar, not salt. Suffice it to say I *love* them both and will continue to taste-test my way between popcorn with salt and popcorn with sugar until I come up with a winner. But the downside of all of that popcorn on Main Street? The many birds that swoop in to eat what doesn't make it into guests' mouths.

I started getting calls and notes to come see departments that Louise and I didn't even have on our list. When one of those calls came from Pest Control, I just had to go. Who *does* manage the popcorn-eating bird population? And what about other popcorn-eating creatures? Pest control at a theme park might seem just too disgusting to think about. So not true. It was beyond fascinating. Mice (none with white gloves who walk on two feet, of course), birds (a bird-in-distress audio file played occasionally over the speaker system), and swampland mosquitoes (controlled by about 10.5 million other, human-friendly bugs)—we dealt with it all while searching for effective, environmentally friendly, preventative, and proactive pest-control methods. These cast members, whom I called Disney Cowboys or Pest Wranglers, were some of the most creative I've ever witnessed in the ways they worked to prevent any interruption (*Swat! Slap! Itch!*) of our guests' magical moments.

Digital Audio-Animated Control System (DACS): Say That Again? And Again? (And Again?)

Just try and imagine It's a Small World *without* music (even if sometimes you wish you could). Or consider the Haunted Mansion without its scary sounds. Really, what would be the point? Underneath the castle in its maze of tunnels (which we actually call utility corridors, or "utilidors") is a place called DACS. Years ago DACS was show and audio mission control with the reels and reels of sounds and music that would bring parades, attractions, and shows to life. The department also managed lighting and fire protection systems and the synchrony of hundreds of audio-animatronic figures. Of course, that technology has changed dramatically. Today it is a *huge* computer operation, but the point remains the same: behind the scenes is where the magic begins. The DACS team were some of the smartest, detail-oriented people on the planet. They had to stay on top of every little noise, movement, and action around the park to ensure the best possible sensory experience.

Horticulture: Not Your Garden Variety

The Disney theme parks feature some of the most beautiful landscaping in the world. When you arrive at the Magic Kingdom, you are greeted by Mickey's floral face (itself tended nightly and replanted with tens of thousands of bedding plants through the year), and throughout the parks you can see trees and shrubs in the shapes of all of your favorite characters. This isn't happenstance, of course, but who knew just how much happens behind the scenes in the horticulture department? Not me, that's for sure.

And they said I couldn't cut it in landscaping.

An entire departmental area was dedicated to soil. Planning was required years in advance to display "show-ready" landscapes in optimal maturity to set the scene. And this involved engineering, maintenance, and design to determine every kind of planting in every season, for every precisely plotted location in and around the park's four thousand acres of landscaped . . . swampland!

That's the equivalent of three thousand football fields manicured and beautified with some thirty million blooms. The Horticulture Department was a city bursting with talented people buzzing around every day to ensure that flora and foliage were not just park accents, but art in and of themselves. This area eventually got its own celebration, and now every year Epcot hosts its International Flower and Garden Festival. It is a sight to see (and smell), but I was even more amazed knowing "the dirt" behind the scenes.

Castle Magic

Right from the start, I've had a fascination with Cinderella Castle. Our family vacations to Walt Disney World always began with a stop at the castle, where we would stand on Main Street and take it all in before walking through the castle to Fantasyland. On that first day, it was important to stay until dark and see the castle at night, truly the most magical time of all. As I gazed at it, I always wondered what was upstairs and what was happening below.

Upstairs

One of the first things I learned in my Disney training was that the castle's upstairs had a rich but unexpected history. Originally the castle was to have included a suite for Walt, but when he died before Disney World opened, those plans never materialized. Instead, at its 1971 opening, the upper floors of the castle housed telephone operators. I loved knowing that the voices from Disney to the outside world came straight from the castle.

Also on the second floor was King Stefan's Banquet Hall (a full-service restaurant later renamed Cinderella's Royal Table). Today it houses an ornate suite that can be occupied by one family per night and is reserved for special occasions and celebrations. When I joined the company, the upstairs was mostly storage and communications gear. I'm not sure what I was expecting or what would have delivered on my childhood imaginations of castle living, but it certainly wasn't boxes and equipment. Early on, I learned that much of Disney—and life, in general—is a lovely façade that conceals magic-making machinery. And you know something? That's okay. Function has a beauty all its own.

Underneath

To talk about the castle's undergrounds, I first have to explain that Main Street, U.S.A. is on a second-floor level and parts of Fantasyland and Cinderella Castle are actually on a third-floor level of the park. Since the park is positioned on swampland, it could have no underground floors. So the earth that was removed to construct the Seven Seas Lagoon created the raised platform for much of the Magic Kingdom.

Underneath the first level is a labyrinth of "utilidors" that Disney insiders just call tunnels. Color-coded so cast members know where they are in the park, the tunnels are bustling with people and activity, with no hint of the Magic Kingdom's inner workings intruding on the magic happening above. It's a virtual underground city complete with offices, miles of ductwork, pipes and wiring, and fascinating support areas like DACS and Key Control. True beauty runs deep, sometimes far below the surface.

Dressed in Birthday Best

For Disney World's twenty-fifth birthday, that beauty beneath the surface was matched with beauty that floated just on top. Cinderella Castle was transformed from castle to cake. The entire eighteen-story structure was frosted! With four hundred gallons of pink paint, twenty-six candles (twenty-five and one to grow on) that were twenty to forty feet tall, fifty gumballs, thirty lollipops, six-foot stacks of lifesavers, and assorted sprinkles, stars, and gumdrops, the castle was transformed in celebration. The challenge of the operation was threefold. How could Disney World create a colossal confection (1) on a budget; (2) quickly, so as not to interfere with guest visits, and most importantly; (3) carefully, so as to avoid any damage to the Castle's structural integrity?

I had a firsthand account of the challenge because, at the time, my big brother, structural engineer Chip, was the project manager, executing a spectacular plan conceived by my friend amazing Alice (Norsworthy) and the magnificent marketing team. The team devised a plan to coat the castle in paint, adorn it with one thousand square feet of structure-saving inflatable icing, and sprinkle it with candy-coated whimsy. The castle wore its birthday finest for over a year. Once the frosting was removed, it became again the familiar centerpiece of the park. No castle was harmed in the transformation.

Backside Beauty

That just sounds wrong, doesn't it? At Walt Disney World when you walk through Cinderella Castle, you enter Fantasyland. (That is, if there isn't a show going on. During performance times, you have to walk around it. That old tour guide in me has to be specific on that point.) When you exit the castle, you immediately encounter Prince Charming Regal Carrousel. Main Street, U.S.A. is behind you now—just a pleasant, popcorn-scented memory—and you're immersed in the sights and sounds of Fantasyland.

My tour guide training kicks in here again as I send you off with these words: Enjoy your castle dreams. Love a good castle (and, by all means, make the journey to one a priority), but don't be too concerned with what is upstairs. Make sure your castles are supported with substantial underpinnings, and don't be disappointed when your journey pulls you through the castle door and out the other side, because the castle may not be your final destination but rather a gateway to greater adventure.

Around the (Disney) World

In my official capacity of visiting every department on the Disney World roster, I quickly learned that each one required highly specific expertise and training, but some themes were common to all the departments. There are universal ingredients to making magic, yet surprisingly enough, they aren't all that magical. They're actually available to us all, and I consider them the five keys to the kingdom:

⚷ *Work Hard*

Sounds simple, and we hear it all the time. But you know what? It's true. There wasn't one area of Walt Disney World that wasn't full of hardworking cast members dedicated to making dreams come true. It was evident, you *can* work your way to magic. And this was the case regardless of how much their efforts were visible to guests. They were experts in their fields committed to being the very best, and it showed.

Work can be an expression—and more. It can be passion with purpose. It's not all of who we are, but it's an important part of our story that we can communicate to the world around us.

⚷ *Pay (Rapt) Attention to (Minute) Detail*

Disney has always been known for its attention to detail. Whether at the movies or in the theme parks, you might not notice the individual details, but as they come together, they transport you to a land of completely plausible make-believe.

When I think of details, I think of the stunning landscapes of Yosemite (one of my favorite places). You can isolate all the details—clouds brooding over the Sierra Nevadas with waterfalls racing down the mountainside to crash into rivers below. Foreground meadows ablaze with wildflowers and swaying grasses, all painted in colors so saturated and vibrant your eyes can hardly take it in. Alone, each detail arresting in its beauty, but as a mosaic—breathtaking. Details are like that. They are the brushstrokes that make the painting glorious.

I can't think of paying attention to the details without thinking of my former boss, CEO Michael (Eisner). When he was leading the company, he was sometimes criticized for being a micromanager. But I never saw it that way. Michael was like a kid who wanted to know how everything worked. He had an insatiable curiosity and a great capacity for minding the details. He didn't insert himself to take over, but to better understand and encourage the folks performing work that fascinated him. I considered his curiosity and attention to detail among his leadership strengths. His enthusiasm and total engagement brought out the best in all of us. He really wanted to know what the curtains would look like in our resort rooms. He wanted to experience their opening and closing as guests might. Whenever we visited the parks together, we would lose him. Later we'd find that he'd been backstage in a kitchen talking with the chef or trying to get into the closed-off areas to get a look at new construction. (Several times he ended up in the company of Security, needing to produce his name identification or be thrown out for trespassing.) Funny, what Michael was criticized for has become a Disney distinctive. Disney "overmanages details." And organizations around the world now send their leaders to Disney classes to learn how to do the same.

So, here is a good place to pause for a brief Public Service Announcement (P.S.A.). I am often asked the key to Disney magic and I respond with my spin on this acronym that I developed through the years. "P" is for People; success always starts and ends with people (see chapter 5). "S" is about the very important Story (see chapter 4). And finally, it all comes together with "A," Attention to Detail. Simply and profoundly there are no shortcuts. Whether in business or life remember: P.S.A.—People, Story, and Attention to Detail will NEVER EVER lead you astray.

⚷ Get Curiouser and Curiouser to Get Creative

From curiosity comes creativity. Are you trying to solve a problem or make the most of an opportunity? Whichever the case, when you are interested and engaged, those sparks can ignite the true fire that is creativity. As I moved around the company, I bumped into creativity at every turn. (I mean, come on . . . Disney.) And I don't mean just the animators bringing characters to life or imagineers designing new attractions, but also cast members in Key Control and Pest Control making everyday magic. Painted on backstage walls and printed on cast member communications, Walt's words, "Think, believe, dream and dare," were a rallying cry to encourage cast member creativity throughout the company.

Interestingly, in the same way that passion sometimes seems lofty and unattainable, creativity can seem intimidating. It's a word that implies inborn artistic talent. But the creativity that comes from curiosity is a lot more nuts and bolts (or locks and keys) than that. Curiosity-stoked creativity is about seeking, discovering, and doing. Isn't it natural to be curious? And it always leads to creating—or to building and growing something that can be astonishing. What I learned in my travels is that cast members, no matter where they worked, are curious by nature. The magic starts there.

⚷ *Demand Quality*

No shortcuts, no quick fixes, and no compromises. If that could be an anthem for life, you couldn't write a better one. Quality is about constancy—doing something well again and again and again. You can't always articulate what quality is all about, but often you can define it by its conspicuous absence. You can fake quite a lot, but you can't fake quality. Aristotle had it right when he said, "We are what we repeatedly do, and excellence then is not an act but a habit."

Disney is habitually excellent. And this habit is nurtured among cast members who believe the best performance, production, or product is the next one. They never stop trying to have a more productive or a more creative day than the one before. I think that's why Walt was always eager for tomorrow.

⚷ *Have Fun*

Hard work seems an obvious ingredient to magic making, but the often overlooked, undervalued secret ingredient is fun. The cast members around Walt Disney World just seemed to be having fun. Really? Street sweepers are having fun? (Realize that this fun at Disneyland amounts to thirty tons of trash per day, or ten million pounds annually, much of it mastered with one thousand brooms and three thousand mops.) Now don't confuse this "fun" with a happy-clappy, love-every-part-of-every-day of any job you do, but instead, that conviction that you are adding value, that you are creating something of worth.

Fun happens when work satisfies and when the workers find dignity in what they do. Take, for instance, moms and dads. Do they get excited with every diaper change? Are they cheering while refereeing sibling squabbles and all-out wars, or loving dinner prep after a crazy long day? Absolutely not. But are they nurturing, building, and creating something magical? Absolutely. Positively.

Know Your Worth

Beyond the five keys to success in any kingdom, my ambassadorial tour taught me that any role, onstage or backstage, can summon the best of our talents and abilities. Every role can become more than it seems. It can become a calling. Martin Luther King Jr. said it beautifully when he spoke these words to a group of junior high school students:

> And when you discover what you will be in your life, set out to do it as if God Almighty called you at this particular moment in history to do it. Don't just set out to do a good job. Set out to do such a good job that the living, the dead or the unborn couldn't do it any better.
>
> If it falls your lot to be a street sweeper, sweep streets like Michelangelo painted pictures, sweep streets like Beethoven composed music, sweep streets like Leontyne Price sings before the Metropolitan Opera. Sweep streets like Shakespeare wrote poetry. Sweep streets so well that all the hosts of heaven and earth will have to pause and say: "Here lived a great street sweeper who swept his job well."[1]

Walt also believed in the potential inherent in the simplest things. After all, he created a kingdom with a mouse. And Walt knew that hard work could unlock the door to great opportunity. That's likely why he said, "Get in. Not choose, but get in. Be a part of it and then move up. . . . Get in while you have a chance to and at least look and see, and out of it might come something."[2]

I unearthed my journal from that year that taught me how significant and sacred is the life's work of people all around us. From pest wranglers to towel artists and everything in between. I was impressed. Just count the o's. Soooooooo impressed.

Having such fun meeting the cast all over property, how humbling, what an honor, and oh soooooooooooooooooooooo AMAZING!!! I am realizing how hard everyone works––housekeeping about did me in. The folks in the mail room are on the run all day. Central Reservations; phones ring constantly. Oh my, the central laundry, hundreds of thousands of costumes. Everyone was so nice and loved having visitors. When they explained the work they did and with such pride, it made me all the more proud to call myself a cast member. Okay, tomorrow it is pest control: 4 a.m. call time. Hello alarm and double alarm . . . .

My deep hope is that when my fellow cast members consider the worth of their contributions to Disney magic, they won't wonder even for a moment, "Who knew?" I hope they'll be able to say to themselves—*I knew.* And now, so do you.

WHO KNEW?

* When Walt Disney World opened in 1971, daily admission to the Magic Kingdom was $3.50. Before 1981, attractions required tickets for admission. They were labeled A through E. The E tickets were assigned to the newest or most popular attractions such as the Haunted Mansion.

* Every year over three million flowering plants are put in the ground at Walt Disney World. The horticulture department maintains over two million shrubs, 13,000 rose bushes, and 200 topiaries.

* Walt Disney purchased the original forty-three square miles of Central Florida land (mostly swamp land and orange groves) for $5 million, or roughly an average of $185 an acre. The earliest land purchases cost as little as $80 an acre. The last cost $80,000 an acre. To maintain secrecy Walt called this initiative "the Florida Project" or "Project X."

* It is estimated that more than ten million hamburgers, seven million hot dogs, nine million pounds of french fries, and more than fifty million soda pops are consumed yearly by hungry, thirsty Walt Disney World guests. (And, sending a little love to Disneyland by way of a little-known food fact—The Frito-lay owned Frontierland restaurant, Casa de Fritos, was the 1964 birthplace of Doritos. These snacks, repurposed by cutting and frying stale tortillas, became so popular Frito-Lay sold them nationally just two years later. Disneyland=Nacho Mama. Who knew?)

* Walt Disney World is the largest single site employer in the United States, with more than 74,000 cast members.

* More than 20,000 different colors of paint are used at Walt Disney World, and some of the paint on the castle spires and carousel is actually gold leaf.
* Each year enough Mickey Mouse ears are sold that if placed ear to ear they would span 175 miles.
* You're never more than thirty steps from a trash can in the theme parks. In the early days, Walt and the team calculated the number of steps someone would walk before releasing the trash they held in their hands.
* Cinderella Castle is made mostly of fiberglass to look like stone bricks. If you notice, the bricks and windows get smaller in its upper reaches. This is called forced perspective, and it makes the castle look taller. The castle is 189 feet tall, just shy of the 200-foot limit that would have required it to have a blinking red light on top to warn aircraft. (That would never do.) Oh, and its proper name is Cinderella Castle, not Cinderella's Castle.
* If you look carefully at the Roman numerals in clocks around the Magic Kingdom, you'll see that the number "4" is shown as "IIII" in some places and "IV" in others. Disney imagineers knew that "IV" was not commonly used until after the Colonial period, so the faces of clocks in places and attractions set in that era or before use "IIII." Talk about attention to detail!
* And while Disney wants guests to notice details, there are some views Disney prefers to hide in plain sight. You know, mechanicals, doors, trash cans, and fire hydrants. Disney has a solution for this. The solution is paint—in the versatile hue "Go Away Green."

* If you stayed in a different Walt Disney World Resort room every night, it would take you more than seventy-five years to stay in all of them.
* Since 1971 the Walt Disney World monorail trains have logged enough miles to make thirty round trips to the moon.
* Walt Disney World decorates more than 1,500 trees every Christmas season. More than 150 tractor trailer loads of decorations are used to make the "World" merry and bright.

CHAPTER 9

ENJOY THE RIDE
Get in Line and Hold on Tight

Did you know that you're more likely to die falling out of your bed than riding a roller coaster?[1] (I'm thinking these odds change if you are a cast member riding coasters after sandbag testing but before the guest-ready decree. But let's not dwell on that.) You see, roller coasters are much safer than your fear would allow you to believe. You know the *clickety-clank* you hear when you climb that first near-vertical hill of death? That's not the sound of a rickety, threadbare chain straining to haul your body to the top; it's the sweet sound of a safety mechanism that stops you from rolling backward.

The wonder of the roller coaster is that we wait forever in line to willingly hop on something that we imagine could *possibly* kill us—or more likely, make us sick. We climb in, buckle up, check the safety bar one more time, and then we're off. New sights, sounds, and unforeseen experiences hit us with astonishing speed. One moment we're inching up the ascent, adrenaline pumping. We briefly exhale at the top before plunging downhill, catching a little air between the coaster's seat and our own in the descent.

Sudden turns throw us against the side of the car and into each other—and then we're rolled upside down. We suppress occasional waves of nausea. We might even want to get off the ride, if only we knew how. But as we pull into the loading platform, typically three minutes later, we look around to discover we've made it! We catch a breath, have a laugh, and shake off some lingering jitters. And then we get in line to do it all over again.

If there is a better metaphor for life (or a more clichéd one), I don't know it. I could have been the anonymous author of this thought: "Life is a roller coaster. You either can scream every time you hit a bump, or you can throw your hands up and enjoy the ride."

Get in Line

Every adventure starts with getting in line—making the decision to go for it. Each day we wake up, make the decision to get out of bed (remember, possibly riskier than riding the Rock 'n' Roller Coaster), and then we make additional "get-in-line" decisions throughout the day. Some of those are inconsequential and routine; others are more significant, requiring more conscious thought. Regardless of the relative magnitude, we decide every minute of every day to get in line. Over and over and over again.

If you're someone who craves control—and to a great extent, I think we all do—then your consciousness of even the smallest decisions allows you to participate in life with your eyes wide open. We all have some authority over the choices we make. The opposite of this conscious control is *reacting* to all the interruptive, distracting, and sometimes frightening decisions that scream for our attention all day long. When we react, sometimes blaming our emotional responses on the thousands of decisions vying for a nanosecond of our attention, we hand over control. But there's a third possibility—a choice other than seizing control or merely reacting. We can choose to stand beside the ride just out of line to consider our options. By watching the faces of coaster riders and the mechanics of the cars as they whir by, we think we'll find ourselves better equipped to decide. And we wait. And ponder. And wait some more.

In his book *Just Do Something*, Kevin DeYoung talks about the difficulty of decision making in a glut of choices. (Do you want fries or apple slices, sweetened or unsweetened tea, ketchup or mayo, and have you thought about pickles?) We suffer anxiety and paralysis over limitless options, fearing that among the many options available to us, we might make a poor choice. DeYoung shares that the word *decide* originates from the Latin *decider*, meaning "to cut off."[2] Yup, if you get in line for California Screamin', you might miss the three o'clock parade. But here's the thing—if you stand out of line, agonizing over your decision, you're going to miss the parade anyway.

Deciding not to decide is *itself* a decision. If you're not in, by definition you're out! As DeYoung says, we can be ". . . full of passivity and empty on follow-through. We're tinkering around with everyone and everything. Instead, when it comes to our future, we should take some responsibility, make a decision and just do something."[3] In other words, get in line or get moving to the next adventure.

Personally, I want to get in line, seize the moment, and go for broke. Dick (Cook), the beloved hit-driving, creative head of Walt Disney Studios at that time was my best teacher on the subject. He was all in—always! His philosophy about Studio projects was this: "Why do it if we're going to do it halfway?" That philosophy shaped everything from a film's initial concept through production, distribution, marketing, and promotion. If Dick gave a green light to a project, rest assured, it would not be derailed. We were going for a hit. (As someone who started his long Disney career running Disneyland locomotives, Dick knew something about keeping things on track and engineering a success.) He taught me to show up, jump in, and do my part to make it great.

What if you decide to ride the coaster—but wait . . . there's more than one line? Most roller coasters in Disney theme parks offer riders three lines. (Seriously? *Another* choice?) You may select the customary line, the long one you mosey into with your entire group. Then there's the FastPass line, which requires advance planning to acquire said FastPass and return at the appointed time. Finally, there's the single-rider line reserved for the solo adventurer riding the coaster for the twentieth time. I've spent time in each of these lines and decided there isn't a right or wrong one. The ride is still just as exhilarating. So get in line. Any line. You won't regret it. Take the job, wander the unbeaten path, enroll in the crazy class, order something you've never tasted before. Be open to the possibilities.

Love the Line!

Having chosen to get in line, do you love the line? Likely not. We like to hate lines. They're too long, too slow, and we're just so hot and tired. Massachusetts Institute of Technology professor Dick Larsen—nicknamed Dr. Queue—is the guru on all things related to line waiting, including something called "queue rage." He says queue rage happens most often when people sense unfairness—when someone jumps ahead in line without waiting their turn. Dr. Queue is quick to praise Disney because our theme park attractions tend to overestimate posted wait times. And when your wait is shorter than expected, you win.[4]

Over the years, I've learned to love the line because waiting has a purpose. For me, queue rage is more of "queue engage." I've learned to appreciate the anticipation, as well as the preparation and introspection that accompany waiting. In the waiting, I am teachable, and during those teachable times I consider possibilities I might otherwise have hurried past. When you wait, you dig deep. You question (which is a *good* thing), you wonder, and you also might pray. During the waiting, I ask for insight, wisdom, and courage for the ride ahead.

Reminding myself to love the line also keeps me from "destination addiction," a preoccupation with the next place, next job, next partner, next *anything*. It's the habitual reliance on this thought: "When [insert what you most want at that moment] happens, *then* I'll be happy and life will be easier. As long as we believe that happiness is somewhere else, it will never be where we are. Don't wish away the wait. Waiting in line can be as much fun as the ride itself. Disney packs surprises for folks waiting in line. You might get squirted with water from a ship captain's tomb while waiting to enter the Haunted Mansion. You could spy Tink as you work through the queue for the Peter Pan Adventure or chat with a sassy Mr. Potato Head at Toy Story Midway Mania.

One of the longest lines I ever loved was the line to meet Anna and Elsa at Epcot's Norway Pavilion. Disney's animated film *Frozen* had just been released and my niece, Curly, like thousands of other little girls, fell in love. She was five at the time and obsessed—truly obsessed—with Anna and Elsa. In Disney World that Christmas, character visits with the sister duo were crazy. Everyone wanted to meet the pair. Since I worked at Disney, and since Curly's family had traveled all the way from Oregon to Orlando, I *had* to deliver the goods. The rest of the family, Baby Mike's, was invited but they couldn't handle the pressure. So Curly and I had to take on Disney World by ourselves.

At last, Curly meets Elsa and Anna. Just as excited—Auntie Jody, photographer.

The two of us hatched a plan well in advance. The night before the anticipated meeting, we set our alarms for zero dark hundred, and set out our *Frozen* wardrobe ensembles. That morning Curly and I made our way to Disney World and got in line to enter Epcot, part of the first group in the park. Hand in hand, we hightailed it through Mexico and straight to Norway. One dad, dripping with sweat from his exertion, beat us to our destination. He had been up half the night to make sure he got there first. The park opened at 8:00 a.m. for a meet and greet which was scheduled for 10:00. By 9:00 the line closed. Guests were wailing, throwing themselves on the mercy of the cast members to intervene. (The big guests, not their children. Serious queue rage.) Curly was beside herself with excitement. By the time it was our turn, she said, "Auntie, I am *sooo* excited I can't breathe. I think I might die." Finally, Curly got her princess pictures and hugs. With stars in her eyes, she laughed and danced. We'll never know, but I wonder if the moment would have been as monumental without the wait? I think not. It was well worth two hours chilling in Norway to witness her joy. (The cold never bothered me anyway.)

Store All Personal Belongings and Buckle Up

Heed the warnings to discard your trash and stow your treasures before you ride—which would be simple if we could easily discern trash from treasure. Take for instance, Disney souvenirs. Some of us are tempted to keep Disney straws and napkins only to discard them later. Mickey Mouse ears, of course, you keep forever. I have my own method for sorting it all out, dividing life's belongings into three categories: treasure, trash, and trail mix.

Here's how I see it. Treasure is what we keep—those precious items, experiences, and memories that make us smile. These are worth preserving because a lingering moment with these touchstones both reminds us of our past and fortifies us for the ride ahead. We all have treasure that evokes memories and love. Joanna Gaines from HGTV's *Fixer Upper* says, "Stuff is home." (Do you love them as much as I do? Among the treasure her husband saves are notes that Joanna leaves in his overnight bag when he travels. Love.)[5] I'm not saying material things can bring lasting fulfillment or deep-seated joy, but every big ride has a souvenir shop—at least at Disney. Every experience offers us the opportunity to select a special remembrance. I have all kinds of treasures, including handmade gifts from my mom and dad, a Disney scrapbook that Fifi made for me, and mementos from the family farm. My largest treasure is my Grandpa Carbiener's "one-horse open sleigh" in a place of honor inside my home. And the littlest treasures are notes and artwork from the many kiddos in my life. Some of my most precious keepsakes aren't things at all, like the wise counsel given to me from my Disney friends and mentors, like Val (Cohen), with a JD degree from Harvard Law and a black belt in smarts and strength of conviction.

As a surprise, cousin Ken unearthed, restored, and covered 900 miles to deliver Grandpa Carbiener's sleigh to our door. Oh, what fun it is to ride and sing . . . .

Oh, the Places You'll Go!

It's hard to believe I'd never heard about this Dr. Seuss book until sister Fifi sent me a copy and said, "You must read this. It is magical and oh, so encouraging." It was her go-to book in her teaching days, and she referred to it often. I have always loved Dr. Seuss for so many one fish, two fish, red fish, blue fish reasons:

One Fish: I think Dr. Seuss is so cool. This man, Theodore Geisel, known as the children's storyteller, had no children yet has influenced millions and continues to do so today. That is so ironically wonderful. Because John Dreyer and I have no children of our own but instead many fabulous babies of family members and friends (ranging in age from one month to their thirties), that speaks to me in a personal way.

Two Fish: After a successful career in advertising, Theodore Geisel turned to writing. His first book was rejected twenty-seven times, but he never gave up. I love that tenacity.

Red Fish: Dr. Seuss spoke to the child in all of us in the same way that Walt Disney created family entertainment for kids of all ages. Geisel said of his work something Walt could have said of his own: "I never write for children. I write for people."[7]

Blue Fish: Seuss wrote and illustrated *Oh, the Places You'll Go!* as his swan song—the last book he ever wrote—while he battled cancer. And what a benediction it was. I hesitate to give away the punch line, but you probably know it anyway: "Today is your day! Your mountain is waiting. So . . . get on your way!"[8]

You can't enjoy or even find your treasure if you don't get rid of the trash. Use this rule of thumb from artist and designer William Morris, "Have nothing in your house that you do not know to be useful, or believe to be beautiful." Stacy has this expression framed in her home. When her folks died within sixteen months of each other, leaving her to sort through their life's belongings as the estate's executrix, she realized, "If it doesn't serve a purpose or bring you joy, let it go." Let go of stuff that weighs you down, saddens you, or clutters your life. Move on. It's okay to hold on to a nostalgic item that reminds you of the people, experiences, and times you loved, but don't drag along the heavy stuff.

That takes care of trash and treasure. But what about the in-between stuff that hasn't yet developed into treasure but isn't exactly trash either? I call this the trail mix, and it's perhaps my favorite part. These are the issues, questions, and experiences that are different on any given day and always all mixed up. Sweet, salty, crunchy, and complex. Trail mix is what we walk with and chew on as we sort it all out. For me it's an ongoing, lifelong pursuit and well worth carrying on the journey. I can save it for now and sort it out later. Trail mix always has treasure potential.

Hold on Tight and Enjoy the Ride

Are you ready? You're about to take a wild ride on a train powered by something other than its own engine. You see, unlike a train, roller coaster cars speed along with momentum generated upon release from a chain lift at the top of a terrifyingly steep hill. Or they're launched—like a rocket—from home base. Regardless of our start, the ride is much the same. We scream through twists and turns and force ourselves to take a look at the view from frightening heights. Sure, we think we'd like to know what's around every bend, but I'm convinced that much of the ride's enjoyment is in how it amazes and surprises us. (Isn't that what Pocahontas would say? "Just around the river bend. . . .") Would you *really* like to know every twist and turn? It's more fun to be amazed and surprised. But *do* expect to be bumped, and maybe a little bruised and sore. Just when you're not certain you can handle another stomach-flipping drop, remember that the biggest drops give us the most power for the upward climb. Or, as I like to say, "Without a hill, there is no thrill!" If you doubt that, recall what it's like to spin endlessly in a teacup. (No wonder the Hatter is mad.)

Wildest Ride: Grand Opening Team

In my Disney career with its twenty-two stops along the way, perhaps the best thrill ride was serving on the grand opening team for Euro Disneyland (or EDL, now called Disneyland Paris). While others were immersed in park construction, our team focused on synergy and four weeks of events that culminated in a grand opening extravaganza for celebrities and dignitaries alike. I quickly learned this assignment would push me to the limit and back—most certainly a launched coaster. Good thing, because we needed some pneumatic power to get to the top of that hill.

For starters, the construction was pedal to the metal to finish by the publicized opening date. The park had been modeled after our others but not duplicated. Imagine the challenge of creating a breathtaking castle (made with fiberglass stones and forced perspective, no less) in a region dotted with the real deal.

Ride Review—Euro Disney

When I returned from my wildest-ride-truned-weight-loss camp, also known as my stint with the Euro Disney Grand Opening Team, I chewed on my experience. This was my takeaway:

* Are there things I would do differently? (Like handing out something other than thousands of size-specific sweatshirts?) *Yes.*
* Did I learn there was more than one right way to do things? (Or, translated, the American way isn't the only right or only way?) *Indeed.*
* Did I stumble? (Like having too few languages represented at the private events?) *Oui, ja, and si.*
* Did I survive? (All ninety pounds of me at opening?) *Yes to that. Never again saw that number on a scale.*
* Did I thrive? (Did this lead to my next job at corporate in Synergy?) *In fact, yes!*
* Did the team make all the difference? *Of course! What an amazing, get-it-done team—a diverse cast of many talented and hardworking people. Many hands, many minds. Yay, team! (Hats off, oh great leader, Philippe [Bourguignon].)*
* Did I make lifelong friends? *Enthusiastically and gratefully, yes! (Big shout-out to fantastic Nancy [Valeri], my partner in the adventure.)*
* Did I gather many treasures (like learning I could do it; finding family ancestors in Alsace; experiencing teamwork on steroids)? *Oh, yes. Lots of them.*
* Was it a ride I will remember for a lifetime? *Absolutely.*
* Will I continue to draw on those lessons and experiences? *All the time.*
* Would I get in line for another ride like this? *No doubt.*

The same challenge played out in developing Main Street, U.S.A. Its beloved Victorian-inspired architectural elements that looked like scenes from Mary Poppins were interesting and unique in the United States, but in Europe, where that look was actually the genuine article in so many towns and villages? Maybe not. So the imagineers rethought and recreated everything from castle courts to hotels and dinner shows for park guests. All of that extraordinary effort pressed up against an April opening date chosen to take advantage of favorable weather and peak tourism seasons. Hitting that date required an infusion of personnel. For the final five months of construction, five hundred of us from Walt Disney World were redeployed to EDL.

Typical rehearsals and opening day preparations were conducted in construction zones. The finished product for opening day was like wet ink on paper. The infrastructure to support the advance team was bare bones, to say the least. (As an example, our accommodations were the Davy Crockett Campgrounds. Nice, but not exactly five star.) EDL was built in Marne-la-Vallée, a small farming town about twenty miles east of Paris. In the birthplace of haute cuisine, finding places to eat late at night when we finished our work was more than a challenge. *C'était impossible!* (An extreme weight-loss program was a preopening byproduct.) We'd assembled a throng of multinational cast members who shared English as a common language. But under pressure, without sleep and in the confusion, we reverted to our mother tongues. And we ar-tic-u-la-ted our words and spoke *loud*, as if volume might improve understanding. We gestured too. (Surprising how many gestures are universal.) It wasn't always pretty or especially effective. All eyes were on this $4 billion project, in Europe second in cost only to the Chunnel.[6]

And not everyone in France was super supportive of Americans, Disney, or Disneyland Paris. (One French writer called the park "a cultural Chernobyl.") The pressure to succeed was ginormous! There were days when I thought I wouldn't make it. The hill was too high and I was too weak and undernourished. But then, you know what? The ride became larger than me. The multi-national, gold-medal team pulled through. The project was complete. And we were stronger for it.

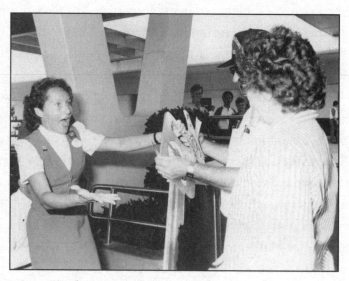

The first car given away in celebration of Walt Disney World's fifteenth anniversary. I may have been more excited than the winner.

Roller Coaster

While I would get in that Disneyland Paris line again and again, there are some drops in life's roller coaster ride that you never forget or can't easily recover from, followed by highs you never counted on. Take the first year I went out for the Disney World Ambassador position. At the announcement ceremony, I stood on the castle stage with the other three finalists. The music played. Mickey presented the roses to the previous ambassador. And then the scroll was unrolled to reveal . . . *someone else's* name. Devastated is not a big enough word to describe how I felt at that moment. My mind raced with what I could have said or done differently in the interview process. My parents and family had flown in for the ceremony, so of course I felt that I had let them down. But then in the depth of my disappointment as I was walking off the stage, I was offered my career-changing job in Marketing. And I was encouraged to try again for the post the following year. Which I got. With a look in the rearview mirror, I can see that I was better equipped a year later, and that year was Disney World's fifteenth anniversary celebration year—all too exciting and a perfect fit for me. As the girl who held twenty-two different positions in thirty years at Disney, I think I've earned the right to say just get in line and prepare to be amazed.

By The Way, Scream!

Do you know the best thing about roller coasters? Roller coasters give you permission to *Scream!* As loud as you can. Don't hold anything back. Yell like you mean it for the entire ride if you like! And don't stop. Live life out loud. Why not? Take a chance on a wild ride that could scare you senseless or make you sick—or possibly give you the best time of your life. Honestly, while the odds are solidly against it, wouldn't you rather die riding the world's greatest roller coaster than falling out of bed?

RAIL TESTING

One of the "jobs" available to those of us in the Team Disney Burbank executive offices was test-riding new attractions. Once the ride was certified for safety, we could become living test dummies, allowing the imagineers to tinker with speed, sound, and other effects before guests would take a turn. Before Disneyland California Adventure (DCA) opened, I took the opportunity to ride the rails all . . . day . . . long. Forgive the indelicacy, but we were human "puke-a-meters." Can you picture riding roller coasters, Ferris wheels, and other moving cars repeatedly, in "casual" business attire, with your boss and colleagues, all without popcorn or soda?

I figured the worst would be the fastest coaster in the new park, California Screamin'. Oh, I was so wrong! That was my favorite. The worst—absolute worst—was the innocuous-looking Ferris wheel-like ride called the Sun Wheel (now called Mickey's Fun Wheel). In one ride, imagineers somehow manage to alarm all of your phobias si-multaneously. Not only does it take you sixteen stories high in typical Ferris wheel gondolas, but it also offers the option of riding in moving gondolas that slip and swing along rails, allowing you to slide from the center of the ride to its perimeter and then back again. You are seated in mesh-enclosed gondolas, so you're not going to fall out, but without a seat belt or harness or even a handle to cling to, you experience every sensation that would tell you that you are, in fact, going to fly off the rails to infinity (and beyond). So disorienting is this ride that it provides guests with motion sickness bags. Now, there's a souvenir for you! My favorite review of the ride was this one: "I have never seen true terror in my wife's face prior to that ride. She tried to find something to hold on to and was so scared, she made them stop on the way down to let

us out. I was laughing so hard and she refuses to go on it ever again."
A close second was the guest who said he'd rather skydive than go on
the Fun Wheel again.[9]

Now imagine experiencing this ride over and over again, seated
next to people you'd really like to impress. If Disney had a hazing
tradition, this could be it. It's worth remembering in life that the scariest-
looking ride could be the one you want to be on. Just going around in
circles can be a far worse fate.

CHAPTER 10

STUCK
Faith, Trust, and Pixie Dust

Hands down, my favorite icebreaker is the one where you write something that no one would know about you on a slip of paper. Everyone then puts those slips in a pile, and one by one, each person takes a slip, reads it aloud, and the group tries to guess who the odd fact describes. I like this exercise because I always know what to write, and I've never met anyone who comes close to matching me in this particular feat. You might be shocked to know that—wait for it—I have been stuck in elevators nine times. *Nine!* Don't believe me? For all but two of those jams, I have witnesses. Most people have never been suspended for any length of time between floors. I grant you, there are some amateurs who have had a little jolt, waited out a long, ten-second pause, and then—presto! The doors parted. I don't even count those.

My elevator story begins before I can even remember. My parents tell me I couldn't wait to get out of my confined space in utero and on with the business of living. (I was ready for the roller coaster.) On a sticky hot Wednesday in July they went racing off to the hospital, Mom in active labor. They arrived minutes later and walked straight through the lobby to the elevator. As happens with labor, one thing led to another, and before they knew it, active labor transitioned to something much more. My mom says she sat on my head as I made my appearance there in the elevator. And so it began.

Have you ever been stuck? Stuck in the mud, stuck in traffic, stuck for an answer? I'd say this is different than decision-making paralysis. This is stuck, most often, not of your own choosing. This jam stops your forward (or upward) progress. You can't move. You can't leave. Usually you can't breathe, but what you *can* do, quite easily, is panic. Will I ever get out? Will it ever end? And will it end well? What should I do next? (Will there be a next?) As I write, I can feel my breath quickening. I'm here to assure you, the *fear* of getting stuck can be worse than actually *being* stuck, especially if you know a few tricks.

Trust me on this. I might be the foremost expert on the subject of elevator stuckness. Let me share my personal rap sheet, the elevators where I have done time:

* A not-to-be named department store (Miami, Florida)
* Rockefeller Center (New York City)
* The Tower of Terror in Disneyland (Anaheim, California)
* A not-to-be-named hotel in Copley Plaza (Boston, Massachusetts)
* The Yacht and Beach Club at Walt Disney World (Orlando, Florida)
* The Team Disney Building (Burbank, California)
* A condominium parking garage (Ft. Lauderdale, Florida)
* Hotel New York at Disneyland Paris (Paris, France)

You can see that, indeed, I have the credentials to speak with authority on the subject. And what I've learned during those periods of suspended animation applies about as well to life as it does to elevators. Let's pry open the doors.

How to Cope When You Get Stuck in Elevators (and Maybe Life)

Number One: Breathe

There are two immediate reactions when you are stuck, and they both result from panic. You either hold your breath or breathe so fast you hyperventilate. Elevator stuckness tip number one: *Don't panic. Breathe.* Continue to breathe normally. In through your nose. Pause. Out through your mouth. I have learned that even after hours stuck in an elevator, oxygen levels are more than adequate, as elevators are not that tightly sealed. In one stucky situation, my sweet dad, the engineer, calmed me with this: if I could see light coming into the elevator car, or if I could use my phone to send a light beam out, oxygen could enter too. So relax and breathe, because not breathing could lead you to pass out. Or worse, it could lead to irrational thinking. And if you're like me, that might not end well. They say the best decisions are made in the worst of times, and the worst decisions are made in the best of times. *Except* when you're stuck in an elevator.

Do you know that stress short-circuits healthy brain functioning? Debra Griest, PhD and executive coach for clients including NASA (talk about being stuck in small places), explains that when we're under stress our fight or flight hormones surge, causing our brain's emotional center to commandeer our brain's thinking center. In stressful situations, with our emotions fully charged and our thinking center hijacked, we can believe all kinds of stuff. Crazy stuff. And if we don't have an answer for something, our supercharged emotional centers will just make something up. *If the doors don't open in five minutes, I will suffocate and die a slow death.* Or, *my husband has planned an elaborate surprise for me and is waiting on the next floor with roses, diamonds, and a string quartet. This is simply part of the ruse.* I can tell you, neither of those scenarios likely is true. But you will arrive at this logical conclusion only when your rational self subdues your emotional self. In the brain, this happens with oxygen. So breathe—deeply.

You'll breathe more easily and think more clearly if you get as comfortable as you can. Take, for example, my unplanned stop in the not-to-be-named Copley Plaza hotel. It was a summer day when the electricity went out and the elevator stopped. I was attired in my Disney ambassador suit, complete with pantyhose, jacket, vest, a buttoned blouse, and heels. The temperature started to rise in that small wood-paneled space, so I started shedding my ambassador's garb. Off went the shoes and the jacket. Then the vest. I might have continued had I represented a different kind of entertainment company. The point is, when you get stuck, get yourself as comfortable as possible. Relax as best you can. Discovering you can get comfortable with being uncomfortable is no small accomplishment. Whether you're stuck in a wood-paneled elevator or in life, some situations are just plain out of your control. You might as well wait it out comfortably.

Laugh and Lead On

The highlight of being a Disney Tour Guide for me was leading the daily tours offered in the Magic Kingdom. We were well rehearsed with a prepared script, but we had also learned lots of additional information so that we could personalize the tour with fun facts and information tailored for a particular group. The tour lasted roughly three hours and included visits to several attractions and a general overview of the Magic Kingdom. On one particular tour about three-fourths of the way through, we'd gathered under a tree to talk about the Liberty Square area. Just then a bird proceeded to dump right on my head and down my shoulders.

I was more than a little surprised and completely thrown off script. Needless to say, we hadn't trained for that moment, and I got the giggles. I ran quickly to the nearest restroom; after all, a well-trained tour guide knows where the nearest restroom is at all times. After wiping off as best I could, I headed back to the group. We all had a good laugh, everyone told their stories about similar bird encounters, and off we went to finish the tour. Here's the truth. That tour stands out in my mind as the best tour ever, certainly the most memorable. I received the nicest guest letter of my tour guide career from a mom who wrote to say what a fabulous lesson it had been for her kids to see me laugh at myself, move on, and continue leading an entertaining tour for everyone. In the years ahead, memories of that tour would remind me not to take myself too seriously. Laugh with the best of them, and always expect the unexpected!

Number Two: Connect

As soon as you've started breathing naturally again, the next priority is to get connected. Whether stuck in an elevator or at a personal impasse, we tend to withdraw. But we need just the opposite. My longest stint in an uncooperative elevator was in the Team Disney Burbank building. Here it's helpful to note that most elevators have an emergency phone—not all of which actually work, FYI. In this case, thank goodness it did. When I picked up the phone, the call went immediately to Disney Security Command Center. The kindest voice ever answered, saying, "Hello, this is Armando." I introduced myself and my situation. Armando (Romero) replied, "Well Jody, I am here for you. I am your lifeline." (I think the popularity of the game show *Who Wants to be a Millionaire* prompted him to say that. Still, I took him at his word.) He was calm and confident, exuding kindness and compassion as he whispered those eight little words anyone stuck in an elevator wants to hear: "I won't hang up until you are out."

Armando asked me if I was okay, and I told him I thought so, though I was feeling a little anxious. He asked if I was alone, and I said yes. He reassured me that everything would be fine and asked me to stay on the line while he called the elevator service. *This is going well*, I thought. I could hear sweet Armando talking to the elevator guy. And then a glitch. I heard Elevator Guy say he was in downtown LA and would have to make his way to Burbank, a twelve-mile trip that could take anywhere from forty-five minutes to forty-five hours. This sent me into a bit of a panic. (Back to step one. Breathe).

I thought if I could keep talking and stay distracted, I would feel better, so I asked Armando if the emergency line phone was capable of conference calls. "Absolutely," he said. Moments later

I could hear Armando-of-the-soothing-voice telling my husband, John Dreyer, that I was stuck in the elevator. When John Dreyer got on the line with me, he sighed (Eeyore, remember?) and then did his level best to reassure me. I told him if he loved me, he would get me out. He replied, "Now Jody, don't be ridiculous," at which point I heard the tap, tap, tap of fingers on a keyboard. "Are you actually working while I'm stuck in here?" With no shame at all, he said yes. Then I said, "Armando, can you get someone else on the phone? This lifeline isn't working so well for me." So we called my mom and dad. After all, Dad was an engineer. Surely he could help me figure a way out of the jam I was in.

When Mom and Dad got on the phone, Mom spoke out of her long-held "it's all good" philosophy and said, "You will be fine. Buck up. Take a nap." But just as expected, precious Dad stayed on the phone with me for over an hour explaining how elevators are designed and why it was safe and how I could get air. He had been the one to tell me that if I could see light coming into the elevator car, or if I could use my phone to send a light beam out, oxygen could enter too. (As an aside, Dad also called that night *and* the next day to recap all we'd discussed, so if I should ever find myself stuck again, and he wasn't reachable, I would be okay. Now Mom and John Dreyer? Hmm. I'm withholding comment. Emotions firmly in check.)

Meanwhile, Armando-of-the-soothing-voice had called my friends "fairy godmother" Virgie, Beth (Huffman), always first to support and pitch in, and loyal, rock-solid Liz (Grissom), who were also in the building. Virgie went to the floor above where I was stuck, laid down on the ground, and chatted with me through the door crack until Elevator Guy arrived. Liz was there when the doors were pried open, greeting me with my favorite ultra-fizzy soda pop the size of my head. Aren't friends *great*?

All of this took a while because Elevator Guy got stuck too—in traffic. When he arrived more than an hour later and finally wedged open the doors enough to pull me out, along with Liz and the giant soda, were the paramedics (much to my embarrassment.) I think Armando-of-the-soothing-voice had heard the panic in my voice. I tell you this long saga because everyone needs a lifeline (thanks, Armando), pals (Virgie, Beth, and Liz, big hugs to you), family (John Dreyer and Mom, sort of; Dad, love you forever and always), a crowbar (Elevator Guy, you rock), and paramedics (skilled and often easy on the eyes, but not always necessary, thank goodness.). These are the folks who offer wise counsel, comfort, and security. They'll stay with you until you are "unstuck." In those dark times when it feels like things are closing in on you, it's important to get connected and stay connected.

Inside Connections

The upside to getting stuck is the *new* connections you can make. Remember the old Scout song, "Make new friends, but keep the old. One is silver and the other gold"? I was a proud, badge-wearing, top-cookie-selling, "Miss Camp Molly Lauman" Girl Scout, and I love those lines. I have a collection of silver friends as a result of getting stuck. Some, quite literally, are silver.

My second (postnatal) experience between floors, I was with an elderly couple and their poodle. All kinds of possibilities there, right? I have to confess right up front that I am not an animal person. I know. I know. Anyone who loves Disney and spends thirty years as a cast member repping a mouse must love all creatures big and small. Not this girl, and for legitimate reasons. First, I was scratched by a cat when I was young. Second, I never grew up with family pets (excluding the goldfish that Baby Mike rocked to sleep, and one rabbit that we later found out was really a series of rabbits, each a look-alike to replace an expired predecessor). Third, my dad was raised on a farm where the animals stayed outside in pens and barns, not inside on sofas and beds. And the capper is this: just a few years ago in the early morning, my animal-loving husband was attacked in our backyard by a rabid raccoon. And we know it was rabid because John Dreyer wrestled and choked the crazy clawed animal until it was a goner. Animal control confirmed what John Dreyer knew. (Note on John Dreyer: not so good with wives stuck in elevators, but possesses excellent survival and protective skills. Let's keep him.)

Taken together, these incidents explain why I'm not totally comfortable around furry things. So when I got stuck in a small space with a poodle named Poochie, I was less than thrilled. But Poochie had parents, and this couple was such fun and oh-so-interesting. This was the most exciting thing that had happened to them in ages, and they couldn't wait to tell their friends all about it. Poochie's dad was retired from a company that advised startups. We had a fascinating conversation. And I came to appreciate Poochie too. We got that yapper barking up a storm. Eventually someone heard Poochie's distress signals and called the office. (Note: Did I mention, not all elevator phones work? !#@%&*?!^!)

You just never know who you might meet on an extended stay in an elevator. Over the years, people have sent me articles about "elevator encounters," and the marriages that have resulted, new jobs that were secured, and all sorts of friendships that had begun because a stuck elevator occasioned a meaningful connection. Just when you think you'll be trapped forever, you may discover that you've been trapped for good. Such is the nature of shared experiences.

Walt Disney was a champion of teamwork and community. He recognized that difficulties became smaller when shared. Walt said, "We share, to a large extent, one another's fate. We help create those circumstances which favor or challenge us in meeting our objectives or realizing our dreams. (Or reaching the next floor, I would add.) There is great comfort and inspiration in the feeling of close human relationships and its bearing on our mutual fortunes—a powerful force, to overcome the 'tough breaks' which are certain to come to most of us from time to time."[1] Which leads me to a final point on how to cope when your elevator or your life grinds to a halt.

Speedbumps and Brick Walls

I've gathered most of my experience getting stuck on elevators, but maybe you, like many others, haven't enjoyed the same excitement Poochie and I have. Yet I'm quite sure you've hit rough terrain and roadblocks in your life and work. I call these speed bumps and brick walls. Speed bumps slow us down. They make us stop and take notice or prompt us to change direction or perspective. We need reasons to reevaluate and reexamine. Without slowdowns we don't often do that. So take advantage of detours and slight bumps along the road. Remember, as the saying goes, few destinations are reached without making some turns.

Then there are brick walls—those things that stop us in

our tracks. You can't avoid these or skirt around them the way you do speed bumps. They are a cousin of "stuck," but more severe. Chances are, the doors won't open in these situations. You'll have to take down the wall one brick at a time or find another way around. These are hard stops, and they hurt. They often leave a mark. My dad's illness and death was a brick wall for me and for our family. We will never be the same or get over the loss, but we are learning to live with his absence. We are trusting that he suffers no longer in a place where there are no more tears. We will see him again, and maybe the time apart will seem like the blink of an eye. But until that time, we live in peace with an ache that has taken his place and, for me, the sweet memories of a dad who was always able to help me in the tightest spaces and darkest places.

Love you Dad, forever and always.

Number Three: Learn and Grow

Every time I get stuck and then unstuck, I emerge stronger and better for the experience. I have met interesting people in elevators. I have learned how to lean on and trust others. I have developed an appreciation for furry things, and I have learned a lot about myself in tough situations. Walt himself said, "A kick in the teeth might be the best thing in the world for you."[2] When you are tested or stuck, afraid or facing adversity, the only way beyond it is to walk through it. But value those times. I promise, you will grow stronger as you dig deeper. As the saying goes, the taller the building, the deeper the foundation.

When You're Struck, Not Stuck

This is where the rubber meets the road for me, where the inspirational quotes and the pithy sayings are torn away like gift wrap on a five-year-old's birthday present. Life will do that. It'll strip you of pretty wrapping to reveal what's inside. When it does, what you believe to be true makes all the difference. Turns out, my elevator mishaps were merely trial runs for what was to come when stuck became struck.

Before I get to the heart of the matter, a little background on The Walt Disney Company's airplanes. Disney has several company planes. The original was used by Walt Disney beginning in 1963. When Walt was flying back and forth from California to Florida surveying land for what would become Walt Disney World, the airline schedules couldn't accommodate his needs. Enter The Disney Company plane. The first was a twin-propeller plane. It served Walt until 1964 when it was replaced by two others in quick succession. The second plane was a faster twin-prop with an interior design and color scheme selected by wife Lillian. Just months later, that plane was replaced by a turboprop that flew 50 percent faster. Good thing, because Walt and his imagineers logged tens of thousands of miles flying from California to New York for the 1964–65 World's Fair, over central Florida swampland and back again.

In the early years, the plane flew incognito. No need to alert anyone about the acreage Walt was scouting and scooping up under the names of shell companies like the Ayefour Corp., cleverly named after nearby Interstate 4 or—say it aloud with me—the I-4. (Disney World property that was purchased quietly for as little as $80 an acre in 1963 skyrocketed in price to $80,000 an acre when word got out.)[3] By 1967 the Disney turboprop plane was identified with tail numbers N234MM. Pilots would alter the FAA alphabet slightly to refer to it as "November-2–3–4 Mickey Mouse." Later they called it the "Mickey Mouse," or just "The Mouse."[4]

In the 1980s, the plane was emblazoned with the face of Mickey Mouse on the tail. During my ambassador year, we traveled domestically on "The Mouse" on goodwill tours. Excited fans would await our arrival, eager to see the plane and meet the characters I traveled with. That plane had been on display in the back lot of Disney Studios until it was removed to make way for the Star Wars attraction. To this day, there are several jets in the company fleet. These planes are used for a variety of functions, for both domestic and international travel. I was on a domestic flight, just a quick jaunt from New York to California, when the difference between being stuck and struck became clear to me.

Photo courtesy of family pal Myrt Harnack.

No mistaking this plane on the tarmac. We always received attention and a warm welcome from the crowd—especially in my hometown.

Aviation experts figure every airliner is struck by lightning in flight at least once a year.[5] That's a fine fact to know but of little value and certainly no comfort when *your* jet is struck. On this particular coast-to-coast trip when our plane was hit, we witnessed an immediate flash, and then total darkness.

Darkness

The quiet told us what we'd rather not have known. Everything had stopped. Turbo engines, most notably. For what seemed an eternity, we glided. Quietly. What seemed a long time was probably just a few l-o-n-g seconds. Then the lights popped back on and the engines whirred back to business. In that moment of darkness, however, more disconcerting than being stuck on the elevator, I thought, *Okay, what if this is it?* I knew my answer even before the voice of our smart and experienced chief pilot told us the emergency system had kicked in and reassured us we were going to be fine.

When we landed, the aviation team was waiting to greet us. I imagine they thought we had passed out from fright. They and our veteran pilot, Mike (Morris), who was also the unflappable head of aviation, invited us to take a look at the damage. I will never forget seeing the small burn hole where the lightning had entered the plane's aluminum fuselage and the larger hole where it had exited. Mike (Philbeck), aviation scheduler and all-around great guy, said, "Jody, you are so calm. Weren't you scared?"

And here is what I learned from that experience and the other times I've been stuck: you'd better know with certainty and confidence what you believe. I am a control freak by nature, which is all well and good while you're at the controls. But when I've found myself stuck or struck, having to trust in something or someone beyond my control, I learned whether my faith could stand the test. Rather, I learned that the One in whom I had faith could stand the test. Any test. We pray for open doors and light. And while those are inspiring images of hope and guidance, they are flimsy in the face of life's ultimate unknowns. In uncertain times, I have believed that God holds my future in His hands. He numbers my days. Pastor Tim Keller puts it this way: "What we believe about the future is one of the best predictions for how we act today."[6] I had believed that before, but on the plane that day I lived it.

So that takes us from birth to near-death and places where I have been stuck in between. Let's return to birth on the Carbiener family farm, where stuck meets good ol' practical pluck.

Reach in and Pull

First, a short backstory: Uncle Dean was a farmer's farmer with a tendency toward the mischievous. His wife was the practical, no-nonsense, tireless Aunt Karol. Together they shared an abiding love for the farm and its animals. They instilled in the next generation of Carbieners the same kind of reverence for the circle of life in all its guts and glory—sometimes both at the same time.

Uncle Dean of "reach in and pull" fame.

I venture a guess that most people haven't watched a calf being born. Take it from me—it isn't pretty. It's plain awkward. The calf's legs get all tangled and its snout pops out between its hooves, and the whole time you marvel (and cringe) at the size of the baby compared to the laboring cow. In one instance, mama cow was really struggling after a long labor in which the calf had turned breech, or had somehow decided she was not leaving anytime soon. Well, my uncle Dean hunched down and, with greased arms, reached in. He put everything he had into wresting that calf from its mama. The two of them, if you count the mama, were sweating and straining when all of a sudden, out floundered and flailed that slippery calf. Uncle Dean landed on his rear in the final effort, and from that position he turned to me and said, "Sometimes you just have to reach in and pull."

Take that one to the bank. When you are stuck—and I mean panic-inducing, breath-stopping, painfully stuck—you may have to muster all your strength, reach from the depths of your being, and with everything you have—*pull*.

Sure, it would be so much easier if we could avoid being stuck. Or struck. But since we don't have control over that, I encourage you to make reliable connections for just such times, test what you believe, and get to know the One who holds your future. And take a final tip from me—get your priorities straight. If you've learned nothing else from me regarding elevators, make a note: use the restroom before getting on an elevator. Just sayin'.

JUST KEEP DANCING

When I was in the Magic Kingdom College Program, I danced in the Main Street Electrical Parade as a Cinderella ballroom dancer. Part of the Entertainment Department training for the role was what to do when you had an "issue." An issue could be anything from turning an ankle or tripping on your hem to falling off the stage. At that time, we wore the older version of the ball gowns that used battery-powered light strings to bring the costumes to life. One night as my partner, Steve, danced around me, he leaned close and said, "You're smoking." *Why, Steve*, I thought. *Thank you. I had no idea. Even in my leaning-tower-of-synthetic-hair wig?* Then I caught a whiff of a smoldering, spatula-on-burner kind of smell.

Recalling my training and fully aware that spotters positioned on the rooftops of Main Street buildings would be watching, I twirled my smokin' little self right down a side street and through the first door I came to. Once inside, I stripped, dropped, and rolled. With only a slight singe on my side, I emerged no worse for the wear and feeling a greater kinship to *Cinder*ella. The life lesson here? Smile, keep dancing to the best of your ability until things cool off, and if a guy dressed like a prince dances by you and tells you you're smokin', be prepared to make a graceful exit, because these things rarely end well.

CHAPTER 11

OPEN HANDS

Show Your Character

In 1940 and on the eve of a world war, moviegoers were introduced to a little puppet made of pine that granted the gift of life in all its fullness—promise as well as peril. All because the toymaker Geppetto wished upon a star. "When you Wish upon a Star" was Walt Disney Studio's first Oscar-winning song, and it remains the company's theme song. And why not? Disney is all about fulfilling the wishes of children of all ages. A quick look at the company's charitable efforts reveals something of Disney's heartbeat, one that echoes the earliest interests of its founders.

Two of Disney's longstanding charitable partnerships forged under Walt and Roy's leadership include the US Marine Corps' Toys for Tots program and the Boys & Girls Clubs of America. Toys for Tots was actually a local outreach started in Los Angeles in 1947. A year later Walt Disney joined the effort and led the design of the Toys for Tots logo used to this day. (Notice the train. Walt was fascinated with trains, and he spent countless hours tinkering with a large-scale model railroad he built in his backyard.) The Boys & Girls Clubs partnership began when the clubs were only for boys—a safe place for "boys who roamed the streets" to receive guidance that would help them realize their potential. Since those early days, Disney has partnered in all kinds of charitable endeavors that align with its threefold corporate concern for compassion, creativity, and conservation.

I came to know Disney's philanthropy up close and personally when I became head of DWO, Disney Worldwide Outreach, and was charged with organizing our charitable giving—of volunteer time, in-kind donations, and money—around Disney principles and values. If I were to pull the thread that knit together the diversity of our efforts, it would be a common wish that children and families would find hope and happiness. Hope in situations that seem beyond hope, and happiness for those who needed it most. The cause that has come to represent this more than any other is wish granting for children with life-threatening medical conditions. Disney's partnership with Make-A-Wish (the world's largest wish-granting organization) is evidence of that. Since 1980, Make-A-Wish has granted the wishes of children with life-threatening medical conditions, and Disney has participated in over 100,000 wishes as the organization's most-requested wish. One of every two wishes granted by Make-A-Wish are fulfilled in partnership with The Walt Disney Company. As much as any of us want this sort of Disney program to dry up for lack of these special guests, as long as there are children and families needing some happiness and smiles during painful times, Disney is ready to deliver. What a privilege.

Disney is an organization chock-full of compassionate cast members, inspired by a bighearted mouse with open hands. Really. Have you ever looked at Mickey's hands, each one with three fingers and one thumb? Walt said that downsizing Mickey's digits to only four prevented his hands from looking like a bunch of bananas, and it saved the company bunches at the same time. "Not having an extra finger in each of 45,000 drawings that make up a six and one-half minute short has saved the Studio millions."[1] I'm more interested in the implications of the simple physical characteristic of Mickey's open hand. Maybe you'll remember from our look into Disney's guest service practices how theme park cast members are trained to gesture with a full hand or to point with two fingers, never one. Disney pays attention to the hands. You don't see characters in the parks with clenched fists or tightly crossed arms. Even villains practice friendliness by making eye contact and keeping their hands (or paws) and arms open. That's not only a great way to approach guests, it's a great way to approach life—with open hands ready to welcome and give.

Look around with Eyes Wide Open

Great news! We are not alone. We are each set in community, and I believe purposely so. Just look around—your neighborhood, your workplace, the areas you touch near *and* far. That, my friend, is your playground for outreach. In the early days, Disney discovered a playground in their neighborhood, a place that could use the kind of magic Disney had in abundance. From the late 1920s through the 1930s, Disney regularly dispatched artists and animators to the nearby Children's Hospital of Los Angeles to draw pictures to entertain and comfort the children there. That kind of neighborly involvement continued when the studios moved to Burbank and Walt established a close relationship with a local children's hospital, which extended to hosting a Christmas party and show for the young patients and children of hospital employees. In the 1960s, as Disneyland moved into the Orange County neighborhood, Walt again contributed to the community by spearheading (with Walter Knott of Knott's Berry Farm) the development of Children's Hospital of Orange County. Their mascot, Choco Bear, is the creation of a Disney artist. From the earliest days, Disney has followed the passion of the company and its founders: the happiness of children.

Sharing Joy in the Journey

Cars is the 2006 computer-animated Pixar film that really summarizes enjoying the ride. The overarching theme, that life is about the journey and not the finish line, "drives" the point home. There are friendships, fun, and surprises to be had along the way; in this case, especially in Radiator Springs. The Rascal Flatts song from the movie, "Life Is a Highway," captures this feeling with the lead line, "life is a road that you travel on," just like that roller coaster. If you don't believe me, take it from car number 95, Lightning McQueen, and don't be too focused on the race that you miss the magic in between. And just as an aside, do you love Mater? I do, and I love the voice of Larry the Cable Guy too. During the week of the *Cars* premiere at the Charlotte Motor Speedway, he visited the local children's hospital and had the kids roaring with laughter. As a matter of fact, we couldn't get him to leave. He even let one little boy who was having trouble enjoying the party smear cake on his face. A real star in my book, just "git-r-done."

Open Your Heart: Love Your Neighbor

Years later, working toward a more disciplined approach to outreach, we discovered an effective litmus test to guide our efforts. The goal was to make the communities where we lived and/or worked better. We took a look at communities around the world where we were doing business and asked, "How can we be the neighbor of choice?" We quickly realized that accomplishing this required a deeper investment as active participants in our communities. Launching a worldwide outreach program shaped up to be a lot like synergy and teamwork but with some extra juice. A renewed and organized focus for our corporate citizenship efforts resulted. Good ol' four-fingered, open-handed philanthropy makes a better community.

Back to the Farm

When it comes to an example of lending an open hand with an open heart, I have only to look as far as our family farm. People in farm communities seem to take individual responsibility for the common good. Joys are shared and sorrows divided in these special places. My dad and his siblings, (reach in and pull) Dean and Evelyn, were born in the farmhouse built by my great-grandfather. It stands today on the family's Bremen, Indiana farm, which isn't something we take for granted. Uncle Dean, a fourth-generation farmer, often retold the story of Palm Sunday 1965 when an outbreak of tornadoes swept through the Midwest from Iowa to Ohio. That weekend forty-seven twisters killed 271 people and injured another 1,500. In Indiana alone, 140 were killed in storms that ravaged northern Indiana and the Carbiener family farm.[2] The winds tore down the barn and ripped through fences and fields. Thank goodness no one was injured at our farm. Others weren't so fortunate.

The Carbiener barn was imploded by
a Northern Indiana tornado.

The Carbiener family barn built in 1900 and the silo collapsed, freeing the bull, which was found later wandering debris-littered fields. Once the storms cleared, in no time at all, people started arriving to help. My family knew many of the folks that would continue to come in the days and weeks to follow, but some they had never seen before. Most notably, Boy Scouts with their leaders from the surrounding towns, tools in hand and ready to work, area churches and the Red Cross providing food for the workers, and clothing and household goods for those families in need.

I was a young girl at the time and I remember Dad waking us up the morning of the tornado saying, "Help your mother and behave. I have to go to the farm," and off he went. He joined the others who'd arrived to do what they could. All of this happened without any cries for help. Folks simply knew to assemble at the scene of the disaster and help where they could.

Let me tell you what that looked like:

* The cows were rounded up and taken to a neighbor's barn. From April to July, the cows were never without a home. Only one milking was missed and the dairy stayed in business.

* The owner of a farm supply and equipment business in nearby Wakarusa moved the milking equipment necessary to milk at the neighbor's farm. No one ever got a bill. (As a result, my grandpa and uncle would never do business with anyone else.)

* Seven long miles of fencing were replaced.

* The image that I most love (as the story has been told to me) is that of saving the fields and crops. The fields were covered with debris, and corn planting would need to begin soon. If planting didn't happen, the feed supply for the animals for the coming year would be in jeopardy and so would the annual crop yield. There was no way to run any equipment until the fields were clear. Walking six or eight abreast, neighborhood kids (most too young for the heavy clean up and rebuild), Boy Scouts, and anyone else available formed a human comb, walking every inch of those fields behind a tractor and flat hay wagon.

They picked up rubble and any useful items from flattened homesteads, which were then taken to a central location for others to claim. This went on for days, in painstakingly slow, methodical labor. A labor of love. The fields were saved with just a few tractor drivers, borrowed hay wagons, some kids and volunteers picking up treasures and debris for families whose lives had been torn apart by killer winds.

All these volunteers, neighbors, and helpers had jobs and farms of their own, but they didn't close or stop. Instead, everyone did a little extra, anything that was needed until the community stabilized. They went where they were needed most. They were community. Look around and I guarantee you will see places where you can jump in and make a difference. Offering kindness to a neighbor will never lead you astray.

With Open Hands, You Have What It Takes

You know by now that I love a practical approach to just about everything in life, and open-handed living is no exception. That begins with a first step that I call "assessing your assets." (Say that ten times fast.) Every business and every person has something valuable to give. You can determine what that is by taking stock of your resources. The discovery of who you are, what expertise you have, and what stores of abundance you can offer will help get you started.

Are you trained in an area that could help someone else? What gifts or know-how have you developed that you can share?

And what about financial support? Checks and cash might be the first thing that come to mind when you think about charitable giving. But don't be daunted if you don't have the dough to donate. I bet you have gently worn clothing, outgrown sports equipment, forgotten wedding gifts, lesser-loved toys, and books you're not likely to read again. Take inventory. This is especially fun to do as a family. Go through the stuff that seems to multiply in dark closets and find a place to donate it—for immediate use or for sale to support a charity you connect with. Taking time to assess your assets will remind you of your wealth, even when you feel cash-strapped. In the process, I guarantee you'll find spare change.

One of my friends and her coworkers have positioned a spare change jar in their department to make much of little gifts. Every month they give the collected coin (and then some) to someone in the company who could use a little help. She said they have had such fun giving it away. Once they gave the money to someone who had suffered a house fire, another time to buy shoes and winter coats, and once to defray a coworker's travel expenses to attend a funeral of a family member.

What You Have, Not What You Lack

You're probably familiar with the Bible's account of Jesus feeding the five thousand on the beach. Here's the summary: John the Baptist, Jesus's cousin, had just been beheaded. The disciples who had buried John's body rejoined Jesus by the Sea of Galilee to share the terrible news. Upon hearing it, Jesus drew away—alone. As He set out in a boat to cross the lake, people from nearby villages followed and walked around the shore to meet Him on the other side. When Jesus saw them, He was moved with compassion and loved on the thousands all day long. As dinnertime approached, the disciples encouraged Jesus to send the people away to get their own food. Jesus resisted, asking, "What do we have?" The answer was five loaves and two fish (possibly from some young boy who might not have been thrilled to share from his brown bag). Jesus then asked the gathered crowd to take a seat. After giving thanks and distributing the undersized offering, five thousand men (and certainly women and children too) were fed and satisfied. So satisfied, in fact, that twelve baskets of leftovers were collected.[3]

Leave it to Jesus to throw a great lakeside picnic. This is what I take away from the story:

* ✸ Jesus needed time alone to deal with grief.
* ✸ He also encouraged time in community. Whether the villagers were seeking Jesus for His healing miracles or had heard the news of John's beheading and were filled with anxiety and grief of their own, they wanted to be in community. Jesus didn't stop that. He joined the gathering.
* ✸ When it came time to fill an obvious practical need, He didn't ask, "What are we missing?" He instead asked, "What do we have?"
* ✸ And He asked the team—not one person—to fill the gap. Don't we love a team? Team efforts multiply results.
* ✸ He invited everyone to sit down. Get comfortable. Join the group. This was not going to be a dine-and-dash event.
* ✸ He gave thanks and then trusted that all they had was all they needed.

Beyond the obvious, physical miracle of the multiplied picnic provisions, I wonder if God was working less apparent (but transformational) miracles in the hearts of those gathered. Did people dig a little deeper to share what little they had? And what about those leftovers? Were people satisfied more completely by the experience of being together? Maybe the food seemed somehow less important. Our Young Life friend Josh (Griffin) believes the miracle was for the disciples. "I bet they had no idea how much food there was to start with," he said. "I think that's even more powerful—that sometimes in the midst of providing for the crowd, Jesus saves the life-changing miracle for his workers and followers closest to him, to encourage and equip *them*." The story tells me that what I have to offer—however scant in my estimation—may be all that's needed. What I have to offer matters more than what I lack.

Open Wide

Once you've figured out what you have to give, the fun really begins. As my favorite money guru, Dave Ramsey, says: "I can promise you, from meeting thousands of millionaires, that the thing the healthy ones share is a love of giving. Generous giving really is the most fun you can have with money."[4] My favorite example of amped-up giving occurred about a year into the creation of Disney Worldwide Outreach. We had spent the year "assessing our assets" and realized that while we did great work with families and children dealing with life-threatening illnesses, there were some deficiencies we could address.

I already mentioned that a visit to Disney theme parks—and meeting favorite characters—is the number one wish of children with life-threatening illnesses. At this writing more than 7,400 wishes are fulfilled every year in Disney's US parks. If you've been a theme park guest, you know how exciting and also how tiring a visit can be, even if you're healthy. For children dealing with serious illnesses, the visit can be extraordinarily taxing. Often they need to stop, take medication, or just rest for a spell. It only seemed natural to create a space for these VIPs, but square footage within the parks is as valuable as pure gold. It took the collaboration of the right people in the right places to make our wish come true (yay, Phil Holmes). So we met with teams from Operations, Parks Design and Engineering, and Facilities Asset Management to discuss how we could better accommodate these precious guests. The result of those efforts are the Disney Wish Lounges equipped with water and cold drinks, throw pillows and child-sized furniture, books, video games, and DVDs to provide our guests a quiet, comforting oasis. You will never see these lounges. They aren't promoted. But they serve a deeply significant purpose. That project still makes my heart happy, and it serves as a prime example of seeing a need, assessing your assets, and pulling together to make something good happen.

Now, I know you're thinking, *But Jody, I don't have the resources of The Walt Disney Company.* What you *do* have are your hands, and those hands can do some mighty awesome outreach once you've opened your eyes and your heart.

Lending a Helping Ham

What do you do when you don't know what to do? Maybe you're aware of a neighbor who is going through a difficult time, but you don't want to intrude or say or do the wrong thing.

I have been freed from my compassion paralysis by a ham—several of them, actually. About ten years ago, a friend shared that when her mom died, so many people showed up to console her that she quickly became overwhelmed gathering and preparing food for the guests. That's when I realized a ham might be the perfect offering for the family and a small way to lighten their load. That friend later sent me a note to say, in a slight exaggeration, the ham was the nicest gift she had ever received. Just what she needed and just when she needed it. Turns out, a little ham can go a long way.

Now when I become aware of difficulties or losses and don't know quite how to help, I deliver or send a ham or a turkey. (Still awaiting that frequent buyer points program.) I'm inclined to think the ham fills the belly and the thought helps mend the heart. One of the precious kids at our church started calling me the "Ham Lady." (Not terribly flattering, but I've been called worse.) When life happens to my friends, they call or email to say, "For goodness sake, don't you dare send me a ham." And then I do. Of course. I'm the Ham Lady. You probably have your "go-to" casserole, soup, or cookie recipe that you make for friends in need. Maybe you like to share by way of a gift card to a local pizza shop. Whatever the comfort, it's nice to settle on your signature expression of support. Mine just happens to be ham.

With Heart and Hands Wide Open, Show Your Character

I sometimes think it's easier to write a check or deposit cash in a bucket than it is to give up my time. That's why I have such high regard for the cast members who literally "spend" their time in community service. Disney operates an incredible program called VoluntEARS, supporting cast members around the world who volunteer hours in local outreach efforts in their communities. The official program was started in 1983. At its thirty-year anniversary, cast members had logged 878 *years* of volunteer service.[5]

My immersion in the VoluntEARS program, led by Disney king of volunteerism Jeff (Hoffman), taught me so many valuable things.

* *Time is a valuable resource that's fun to give away.* Rolling up your sleeves and digging in to do good is energizing and life-giving. The often-repeated cliché is true: You always receive more than you give. Don't know where to start? Consider the pursuits you enjoy and the causes you are passionate about, then look for opportunities to get involved in those areas. You don't have to start big—just start! My schedule has always been crazy busy with lots of travel, so I most often volunteer on one-time projects. Some people prefer a regular and consistent assignment on an ongoing project.

* *The more the merrier, or what's true for parties is truer for volunteering.* This was my second huge observation. When hundreds of VoluntEARS amassed to work on a project, it was a blast! So grab some peeps and go for it. My favorite project with my pals was VoluntEAR back-to-school

shopping. A gang of us—along with about fifty kids—would enter department stores before regular hours and power shop. What a rush, made even better in the company of friends.

✳ *Anytime you can combine your time, talent, and treasure, you have a home run.* This isn't always possible, but in my experience, the deeper your relationship with an organization the better. This is true personally and professionally too.

To illustrate how donations, passions, and business can go together, let's consider a few examples. Take TOMS, maker of shoes, bags, and eyewear. The company started by donating one pair of TOMS shoes to a person in need for every pair purchased. They have extended that business model to provide potable water, restored eyesight, and even safe birthing services for people in economically challenged places. They financially invest and cooperatively partner in a mission to improve the lives of people around the world in a one-for-one giving promise. Company employees work with global outreach partners to deliver these gifts. By combining these efforts, they create more seamless and sustainable partnerships that benefit everyone involved.

Habitat for Humanity is another awesome organization. I not only admire the work they do, but I am also a big fan of Habitat's homebuilder-in-chief, Jonathan (Reckford), a former Disney Development executive. He is the real deal inside and out. I greatly admire Habitat for the community spirit they foster, the partnerships they build with volunteers and sponsors, and the relationships they cultivate among the house recipients and Habitat staff and volunteers. At Disney I had the privilege of working on several Habitat house builds and awareness-building campaigns. Fascinating how, on the one hand, the work is personal and specific house to house, yet the mission is massive in scope and global in impact. That is a hard balancing act, and Habitat for Humanity does it superbly.

The Big Cheese together with leaders of VoluntEARS, Karen Kawanami and Jeff Hoffman.

On a smaller scale, in an equally worthy effort, is the example of my friends from college who own a car dealership. They operate a coffee shop in the lobby of the dealership and donate the proceeds from sales to the local food bank where they also volunteer. What a great way to make it personal, serve the local community, and serve your customers as well. My friends embodied the words of Ralph Waldo Emerson, "The only true gift is a portion of yourself."[6]

So You Say Volunteers Can't Be Fired?

One of the benefits of philanthropic work—or one of its hazards, depending on your perspective—is this: you can't be fired. (FYI: you *can* be transferred.) Only to prove a point am I willing to tell you about my being fired, I mean relocated, as a volunteer. Our church was serving dinner at a local homeless shelter, and my job was to work the line, making sure everyone had plates and utensils and letting the kitchen know when we ran out of food and needed restocking. That particular night the menu featured hamburgers, a few side dishes, and cookies for dessert. We had organized the serving tables just so. Guests were to approach the table and collect a plate and utensils, then buns, followed by the hamburgers before moving on to the condiments, followed by the sides and desserts. In two lines, folks would move down both sides of the table to expedite the process. It was engineered to be a model of orderliness. What could be better than an organized buffet line?

When the doors opened, people streamed in, approaching the table from every direction. Taking food from virtually any point of entry, much to my horror, hamburger patties were put on top of (not inside) buns, condiments were squirted on side dishes. I watched one gentleman put his hamburger on a cookie. For someone who stresses out when cranberry sauce mingles with mashed potatoes at Thanksgiving dinner, this was disastrous. I kicked it into high gear. I had to intervene and help people organize their plates. In the midst of my frenzy, the manager of the shelter approached me and ever so politely said, "Why don't you head to the kitchen and see if they need you in the back?" Shame on me! I was relocated to the kitchen.

Why do I nark on myself? Because I learned a few important lessons about volunteering from my "transfer":

✳ Never forget who you are serving. This isn't about you. *(And oh, by the way, Jody, they were hungry, and food group separation probably wasn't priority number one.)*

✳ Equally important is knowing who you are and looking for ways to use your gifts and strengths in places you enjoy serving.

✳ Last, relax! As a volunteer, you can't be fired. (Well, not in so many words.)

To cut myself some slack, by the end of the night, I had organized the shelter's food pantry. For an organizer with anal-retentive tendencies, oh my, was that fun. Thereafter, whenever we volunteered there, I would go straight to the pantry and the clothes bins to work my magic. Now when I volunteer, I usually find the storage areas or closets and just do my thing. It gives me joy and energizes me, and I guarantee you can have just as much fun doing *your* thing.

The Magic of Your Open Hands

Don't underestimate the powerful difference you can make in your neighborhood, in your community, and in the world by opening your hands and your heart.

I have come to believe that The Disney Company's philanthropic work is simply an extension of Walt's love of children and his personal understanding that life, which is so capable of magic, is often less than magical. Sometimes far less. Walt's nephew Roy articulated this well in his remarks to recipients of Disney community service awards: "When we talk about Disney magic, we aren't just talking about entertainment magic, we are also talking about the kind of magic you do . . . the kind that lifts up lives and restores health, that gives neglected kids a role model or puts food on the table of a family in need."[7]

Roy was talking about the magic that happens when we open our hands and hearts to something bigger than ourselves—something like making wishes come true. Because, as Jiminy Cricket says, "the most fantastic, magical things can happen, and it all starts with a wish."

PIRATE WISH

Honestly, I'm not a fan of pirate movies—or actually any movie that is too dark or overly scary. I can only handle so much drama before moving on to a happily-ever-after or at least some measure of redemption. I tell you this because, unlike the rest of the world, I am not a Captain Jack Sparrow fan. I get it! I'm a freak. I am, however, a Johnny Depp fan, and here's why: many of our wishes come from kids who want to meet celebrities and/or be at the premiere of their favorite movies. *Pirates of the Caribbean* movies were no exception. We had so many requests to meet Johnny Depp and to attend the *Pirates'* premieres that we didn't know how we could possibly accommodate all the kids requesting the same wish for a personal meeting.

With the hope we could come up with some sort of wish come true, we contacted Johnny's representatives and worked with the fabulous team at Disney Studios. (With the full support from Dick [Cook], the Studios' big-hearted leader, who said, "We *absolutely, positively* will make this happen.") I was overwhelmed when we got word that Johnny wanted to meet with each child *individually*, then invite them to attend the premiere as his guests. What a treat it was to see these sweet kids having such fun in the midst of their arduous journeys. During one teenage girl's chat with Johnny, they cooked up the idea of Johnny recording the voicemail message on her phone. When her friends would call, they would hear, "Hey, this is Johnny. Noel and I are chatting just now, so leave a message for her after the tone." Then, of course, everyone would go wild. They had such fun recording and rerecording until they had the perfect message. They even took selfies to go with the effort. What a perfectly executed wish!

I'm no real competition for Johnny Depp.

Now fast forward a few hours. Our guests had walked the red carpet down Disneyland's Main Street. They'd shopped for Pirates swag, and now it was time to be seated in the outdoor theater built for the movie premiere. At this point, somehow in the process of playing Johnny's message on Noel's voicemail probably a thousand times, the message was erased. Noel was distraught. Actually, distraught doesn't describe it. She was shattered—inconsolable. At this point, Johnny was getting ready to go on stage, and all of the celebrities, dignitaries, and guests were already in their seats. But we had to do something. We worked with Security to get word to Dick, asking him to stall so that we could relay a message to Johnny. How did Captain Jack Sparrow respond to our frantic request? Like a prince! "Well, of course," he said, "we have to stop everything and redo that message. It's all that matters right now." And only then, when the message had been rerecorded, did the show go on. I may not love pirates, but I do have a soft spot in my heart for Johnny Depp.

CHAPTER 12

FIREWORKS

Celebrate Everything!

Disney loves a good party and finds almost any reason to throw one. Case in point: when Walt Disney World arrived at one particularly grand attendance record equal to the US population at the time, we had an over-the-top, no-holds-barred celebration. We brought out the birds, the parades, and of course the fireworks! We even made the 242,831,300th guest an honorary citizen. No kidding. I still have the script from that ceremony. Was it a big day? Or did it become a big day because we decided to make it a big deal—and celebrate accordingly? I often say that Disney celebrates the opening of an envelope. Is it Tuesday? *Let's party.* Is the sky blue? *Bring on the balloons.* Truly? Today is your 33rd and 4-month birthday . . . making you 400 months old? *Are you kidding? This is a Mad Hatter's "very merry unbirthday"! Who doesn't celebrate that? We have to have fireworks!*

As the largest consumer of pyrotechnics in the world, Disney celebrates with a bang—lots of them. If you've seen Disney's fireworks shows, you know they are breathtaking, full of color and music, surprise and delight. The dictionary definition of fireworks sums it up well: combustible devices causing a spectacular display (explosion) of light or a loud noise when ignited; used for signaling or part of a celebration.[1] The secondary definition describes fireworks as an outburst of emotion or a display of brilliance or energy. Webster and the Merriam brothers got it right here. As defined, fireworks need a couple of assists to do their thing. They need a reason to launch them, an agent to ignite them, and to be truly celebratory, a group to enjoy them. No wonder special occasions and days at Disney theme parks always end with fireworks.

Disney premiered its first fireworks show in the summer of 1956, a year after the opening of Disneyland. The original show, like others of the time, was created by hand, and cast members touched off the explosives' fuses with railroad flares. (Walt, train fanatic, probably loved that.) Beginning in the late 1960s, Disneyland developed a system that could fire the pyrotechnics electronically, and to that was added a synchronized musical soundtrack. Their early fireworks shows were actually created using the same storyboard technique as animated cartoons. Today the system has multiple launch sites, special lighting, lasers, and 3-D projection mapping technology for painting images on Magic Kingdom castles. Disney operates the most high-tech choreographed music and pyrotechnics shows around, and it has the patents to prove it.[2]

Some of Disney's most beloved fireworks shows are ones you may know or remember: *Fantasy in the Sky*; *Believe . . . There's Magic in the Stars*; *Wishes: A Magical Gathering of Disney Dreams*; and, my favorite, *Believe . . . in Holiday Magic*. And on many nights you just might glimpse Tinker Bell touching off the fireworks as she flies from the spires of the castle.

Celebrate Everything

For me, fireworks declare that life is worth celebrating. Every day is a gift worth opening. And they don't have to be over-the-top, all-out noise and light shows to do that. Whatever the size of the bang, just the spirit of them makes me love fireworks. Smaller sparkling moments like making s'mores around a fire with people you love, a big hug and kiss from one of my babies (no matter the age), gut-busting laughter with friends, great worship, or a themed party will have the same effect. Many of these sparkling moments ignite spontaneously, but others twinkle at the hand of someone practiced in seizing a moment (almost any moment will do) and rejoicing in it.

While I have been the fortunate protégée of more than a few great "celebrators," three of them take top billing. These three, Mom, Tom, and Mary, have a knack for "touching off the fuse" to light up all kinds of dazzling celebrations.

Mom: So Many Reasons to Celebrate, So Little Time

I have to start with my mama. To better understand her party panache, we need a little backstory, because like childhood does for all of us, Mom's early years shaped who she would become. My grandfather Pople worked in the power and utilities business, and he was transferred often. From the time my mom was school-aged until she was college-bound, she never attended the same school for more than two years. Although outgoing by nature, all those moves and many years of being the "new girl" deepened that trait and pushed her to jump in and make the best of those situations and to celebrate anything and everything. To be honest, she admits to scars that came from being that new girl repeatedly—the girl who doesn't know anyone, unfamiliar with the school's social system and its dos and don'ts, the insecure one beginning yet another first day at a new school. Anyone who has made a midyear move into a new school understands. It's not easy.

The positive side of moving a lot? That mom of mine is just plain fun. She knows how to seize the moment. I remember having pancakes and eggs for what we called breakfast-dinner, and Mom turning that into a pajama party. And the parties she created to rejoice over my dad's arrival home from a big trip or when we'd slogged through an especially tough week. And how she never bemoans, "I wish someone would do something about that." She's always willing to be that someone. When she moved most recently and discovered there wasn't a women's club in the community, she started one. Today that Sea Pines Women's Club has five hundred members. She could transform ordinary into extraordinary and emergency into adventure. Not until we were adults did my siblings and I realize those crazy basement parties on stormy days were Mom's way of distracting us during tornado warnings. Given the family's firsthand tornado experiences, she observed the weather warnings. But that didn't mean we couldn't have fun while waiting them out. Mom didn't major in the usual milestone events that most families celebrate. Birthdays were marked with cake and some singing. No big deal. She majored in minor moments—Kid's Day, the first day of summer, or a day when one of her children did something nice for someone. Oh my, that was a cause for celebration.

I remember shopping with Mom who, by the way (together with sister Fifi) hates to shop. I, on the other hand, love to shop.

Because we were always watching our money, shopping with Mom was all about needs, not wants. During one particular mission, a boy from school said hi to me, so I introduced him to Mom. He told her that he was new to school and that I'd been the first person to talk to him and to show him around and had even asked him to sit with my group of friends at lunch. When my friend left, my typically frugal mom turned to me and said, "What do you want as a treat?" I think she would have bought me anything and everything in that store. (P.S. I bought a very cool, but by family standards not practical, pair of clogs.) We celebrated that night and the week to come as if I were the queen (Queen of the Welcome Wagon). That one hit close to home for her and played on her heart strings, but it was *always* the little, seemingly insignificant things that were cause for celebration in our family. These didn't inspire fireworks displays but smaller expressions like signs on the wall, encouraging notes stuffed in unexpected places or taped to the mirror, or a silly costume—just because. To this day, Mom loves a party. Thanks, Mama.

Tom: Dream Big, Plan Big, Go Big

Early in my Disney career, I had a boss named Tom (Elrod). Called a "marketing whiz" by Disney insiders, Tom is tall with a big grin and an endearing laugh. Well, actually, it's more of chuckle—an infectious, come-join-in, happy kind of sound. That chuckle coming from such an imposing stature creates the impression of a gregarious bear wanting you to come play. He is smart, witty, and creative. And Tom always invites everyone to join in the fun. When I started in Marketing (thank you, best boss Bernie [Bullard], the first person to give the new kid a chance),

Tom was actually my boss's boss's boss. He was not only big, he was a big deal.

I observed how Tom was always all-in, embracing the process and the work, and how he liked nothing more than a meeting where everyone was expressing ideas, passionately agreeing *and* disagreeing. Like a stereotypical dinner in a big Italian family, it wasn't Tom's meeting if the conference room didn't reverberate with outbursts, screams, and laughter. Work under Tom was productive and energizing. He showed me how to own my ideas unapologetically. All of them—big and small, good and bad. Under his leadership, I learned how to "leave it all on the field." Fail big if you must, but go big every time, because when you win, you will win big. And if you win as a team, the win is bigger still.

That time in my career was like none other. I am still so honored to have worked alongside accomplished, creative, and enthusiastic marketers. With a shout-out to phenomenal Phil (Lengyel) and the Disney World marketing team, I still ask myself, *What would the MarketEars do in this situation?* I fondly remember the projects we collaborated on, including one under Tom's leadership that took the cake. Literally.

I already told you how we roundly debated the merits of Mickey and Minnie Mouse matrimony. That discussion took place on the advent of Mickey's sixtieth birthday. (And really, if you're still dating at sixty, why get married?) One of the by-products of those meeting extravaganzas when their eternal sweetheart status was sealed was the idea to celebrate Mickey's sixtieth with the world's biggest birthday party. Once that train had left the station, there was no stopping it. Mickey's Worldwide Kids Party was born. The party would be a four-day event spanning three continents, hosting twenty thousand kids. What better way to celebrate than to have Mickey and Minnie host deserving children who otherwise might never visit a Disney park?

Then came the meeting I will never forget. I was not a seasoned executive, though I'd worked in several areas of Walt Disney World Marketing. Tom called me into his office and said, "Jody, you are going to be in charge of Mickey's sixtieth birthday." I must have looked like I might pass out, because he followed up quickly with, "You can do this." Here was a classic leadership moment. Tom knew something about me that I didn't know about myself, and he was willing to give me a shot. More importantly, he was there leading the way, showing the way, and when necessary, ~~pushing~~ catapulting me outside my comfort zone. Park grand openings had not made my résumé at this point, so Mickey's Worldwide Kids Party was the biggest event I had managed to date. Kids—along with dignitaries and celebrities—came from 120 cities around the world, including Moscow, London, Paris, and Munich. We coordinated the travel, lodging, meals, and activities. As with the Disneyland Paris grand opening yet to come, had I known that day in Tom's office the size of the task in front of us, I wouldn't have had the guts to accept the challenge.

What really made the effort worthwhile is captured by the image that I can see clearly even now: lining Main Street were thousands of kids in matching Mickey Mouse shirts, holding signs identifying their hometowns from countries around the globe. We served up birthday cake, which at the time broke the Guinness Book of World Records for the biggest ever, measuring one thousand feet long and roughly in the shape of an M. One little boy said it was the best day of his life because he had never slept in a bed. Can you imagine? Almost none of the children had ever been on an airplane, let alone visited a Disney theme park. Vitaly was nine and traveling with other children from Russia. He said the best part of the trip was that "everybody smiles, the big people too. Everybody." Smiles, the universal language, spoken and understood by a wise nine-year-old. At Disney, *every* day is a day to celebrate.

Mary: Her Parties Were Practically Perfect in Every Way

Now my last inspiration in this area is none other than Mary Poppins herself. *Mary Poppins* was the first "grown-up" movie I saw in the theater. We all dressed up and even got to have popcorn. It was all so wonderfully magical, as were the lessons I learned from Mary Poppins:

* ✱ *Mary "plans in" sugar.* "For every job that must be done there is an element of fun," according to Mary's wisdom. Plan to party, or as I like to say, party-ize the situation. All it takes is a little sugar. Sugar comes in many forms. Sugar can be words, music, games, or, my favorite, a *theme*. When all else fails, make one up. Why not make tomorrow Wear-a-Hat Day, or Take-a-Friend-to-Lunch day, or Organize-a-Closet Day? Or use one of our go-to sugars and pick a person and make that day their birthday. Celebrate the day as their birthday all day long, complete with cake, singing, and maybe a present. Why not? (*Happy Unbirthday to you!*)

✷ *Mary makes the most of rainy days.* Go outside and stomp in a puddle. Or stay inside and get cozy. Rain brings nourishment and refreshment. It washes things clean and makes the sun shine brighter. Need I mention rainbows?

✷ *Mary instructs her charges to seize the moment.* "Let's go fly a kite!" Don't wait for the invitation, the perfect conditions, or a holiday to schedule a celebration. Don't even let the fact that you don't cook stand in the way. I always say that since I don't cook, I "theme." Never met a themed party I didn't like. And those that involve carryout are the best.

Mary's my inspiration. Come on. Sing along . . . "*Every* day's a holiday with Mary."

I adore Mary Poppins for so many reasons. Can we spend just a minute on that bag of hers? It's uber-organized and able to produce what she needs when she needs it. You know, indispensables like floor lamps, hat stands, dancing shoes, and tape measures. And my girl Mary wears a great hat. Don't you love a good hat? Whether a baseball cap, a wool beanie, or a cowboy hat, you have more fun in a hat. Last, and the icing on the crumpet, Mary speaks an encouraging word. I want to be Mary-like in the way I cheer others on. And I aspire to be Poppins-helpful, all the while keeping it simple. Don't ever confuse simple with easy. Simple methods are understandable, doable, and goal-accomplishing. That doesn't mean they're easy.

Party On

Do you need an excuse to party? Or just a new way to celebrate?
Here are a few of my favorites:

* **Turkey Frank Thanksgivings.** In my twenties when we
  worked the closing shift at Disney World on Thanksgiving,
  I'd invite my fellow cast members to celebrate with a
  turkey frank cookout—at 4:00 a.m. Pilgrim and Indian
  attire encouraged.
* **Miss America Parties.** Bring your talent to share and
  amaze partygoers.
* **(The World's Most Raucous) White Elephant Gift
  Exchange.** The elephant could be Dumbo or some pitiful
  Disney discards.
* **Bingo Parties.** For all the family and babies. Let's empty
  Uncle Johnnie's wallet!
* **Christmas in July.** We started singing carols at the homes
  of those who declined the invitation. (We started getting
  really great attendance.)
* **Pizza and Game Night.** Bring your favorite game. Disney
  Headbands, Twister, and Chicken-Foot Dominoes are a
  few of my faves.
* **Bowling Party without Bowling.** Come dressed in a
  beloved bowling shirt, ready to eat loaded nachos.
* **Mulan Parties.** One of my all-time favorites—takeout,
  sitting on the floor, and chopsticks only. Carryout to the
  rescue.

> ✳ **Worst Case Scenario Parties.** Everyone comes dressed in survival gear ready to answer questions from the game (which may have prepared John Dreyer for wrestling a rabid raccoon).

Supercalifragilisticexpialidocious and Other Encouraging Words

Not all of Disney's fireworks are of the skywriting variety. Some fireworks are simpler and behind the scenes.

As I mentioned in an earlier chapter, every new Disney cast member receives a name tag, first name only, most often in the shape of an oval with a smaller oval overlapping it on top. (Something Walt Disney called the "double bubble.") Mickey or some other iconic image appears at the top, and engraved in the center you find the cast member's first name and hometown. This is part of the costume for "on-stage" cast members. Nonpublic departments of the company don't require the daily wearing of name tags, unless cast members visit on-stage areas. In that case, name tags are pinned in place. Even CEO Michael wore a name tag in the parks. I kept backups for him in a desk drawer or in my own Mary Poppins bag—just in case. (The exception to the name tag practice, even for the CEO, were for park visits he made as a dad with his wife and three boys. He flew under the radar on those visits and enjoyed the park as any other guest might. And he always wore a ball cap. I'm telling you, hats make life more fun.)

Disney issues commemorative name tags in celebration of character, park, and company anniversaries. These are highly collectible, and you will see name tags framed in impressive collages in offices all across the company. The name tags commemorate, and they communicate too. They help to tell individual stories about cast members, like those with fluency in multiple languages. The name tags of these people feature additional pins to identify languages they speak. Cast members celebrating Disney anniversaries could note their favorite animated film on their tag. Disney name tags have evolved over time, and they change with the celebration of park anniversaries, like the ones issued for Mickey's sixtieth birthday. Disney knows that name tags are a fun way to interact with others—fellow cast members and guests alike.

Another celebratory program is The Disney Company Service Awards. Every month special pins are awarded for years of service with the company. These pins are placed on the name tag and worn as a badge of honor. The pin for one year of service is the Steamboat Willy, while a cast member marking twenty-five years of service receives a Tinker Bell pin. As the years of service accrue, employees receive a plaque or statue too. And of course there are related celebrations, anything from luncheons to elaborate black-tie dinners with award-winning food, celebrity performances, and the recognition of the award recipients by senior executives. Some locations hold recognition parties after hours inside the theme parks.

Should you see a cast member wearing a name tag in reversed colors—blue tag with white letters instead of customary white tag with blue letters—you're looking at someone who has earned the most prestigious award issued in the parks, cruise line, and Walt Disney Imagineering. The folks wearing these tags are Legacy

Award honorees. These special people are nominated by fellow cast members and recognized for providing outstanding service to guests and contributing to Disney magic. Legacy Award recipients have earned a reputation for regularly exceeding company standards. Engraved in their name tags are the words, "dream, create, and inspire," to recognize how they are "consistently inspiring others, going out of their way to create happiness for guests and team members, and finding new ways to deliver Disney magic."[3] If you encounter one of these cast members, you will find yourself in good hands. You might even get sprinkled with a little pixie dust.

Walt created the first service awards ten years after Disneyland opened to publicly acknowledge those who had labored so hard to make the dream come true. That spirit continues today. These moments are important, not so much for the statues, mementos, and parties, but for the message they send to cast members: You are important. Your contribution matters. And today, we celebrate you.

Saving the Best for Last. The Kiss Goodnight

Perhaps the sweetest firework of all is also the simplest. Just a kiss goodnight. True to form, it doesn't happen every night, but on many nights, guests who linger in the Magic Kingdom after the attractions close may be treated to a presentation affectionately known as Disney's Kiss Goodnight.

This unadvertised, little-known show takes place thirty minutes to an hour after the attractions close. In a lovely farewell, the castle lights up once again. The sounds of "When You Wish upon a Star" fill the air and twinkle lights dance on the castle walls. In a final gesture of hospitality, guests are bid goodnight with these words:

> Ladies and gentlemen, boys and girls, on behalf of everyone here at the Magic Kingdom, we thank you for joining us today for a magical gathering of family, friends, fun, and fantasy. We hope that your magical journey with us has created wonderful memories that will last a lifetime.
>
> Walt Disney said that the Magic Kingdom is a world of imagination, hopes, and dreams. In this timeless land of enchantment, magic and make-believe are reborn, and fairy tales come true. The Magic Kingdom is a place for the young and the young at heart. A special place where when you wish upon a star, your dreams can come true. Until we see you again, have a safe trip home. Thank you, and goodnight.

Mickey finishes the farewell saying, "So long, everybody. See you real soon." And then the music swells in a final chorus to remind us that dreams *can* come true.

Oh my. Honestly, I can't write those words without getting a lump in my throat. Walt knew that every day is a gift to be received, opened, and treasured. Not all days will be red-letter days, but not a one of them will return. That makes each one worth celebrating.

So get out your sparklers and s'mores. Gather your fun hats and party horns, your well-worn jokes and the precious people you can't live life without. It's time to party . . . And . . .

Don't ever forget the fireworks!

The end of a magical day as seen through a young girl's eyes and her Kodak Instamatic camera.

YOU'RE NEVER TOO OLD
(TO LIGHT UP THE SKY)

We talked about Walt always looking for ways to "plus" the guest experience. What could be more magical than an actual Tinker Bell flying above the spires of Sleeping Beauty Castle to set off Disneyland's "Fantasy in the Sky" fireworks show? In 1961 the hunt for a daring Tinker Bell began. By June 9 Tink had been found. Her name was Tiny Kline. The most amazing thing about Tiny? On her inaugural flight, Tiny was *seventy years old*.

Tiny's given name was Helen Deutsch. The young Jewish Hungarian immigrated to the United States in 1905. She began her career as a burlesque dancer, as many Disney cast members do (just kidding). She was performing in a Wild West show when she met her soon-to-be husband, rodeo trick rider Otto Kline. By their 1915 wedding date, Otto had joined the Ringling Bros. and Barnum & Bailey Circus. They had hoped Tiny could leave her immodest profession dancing in the Cracker Jack Burlesque Company "cooch show" to join him in a more respectable life as a circus performer. But just five weeks after they were married, Otto was killed during a performance. Widowed but not without talent or chutzpa, Tiny learned aerial acrobatics tricks, including the "slide for life." In this trick, she would clamp her teeth around an iron bit attached to a wire suspended at great heights and glide across the wire gracefully as though flying. She performed the trick for forty years, including a 1932 theater publicity flight over Broadway. Upon her rooftop landing, she said, "At last, I found a safe way to cross Times Square." Almost. Moments later she was arrested. (Search for the act on the internet. It's worth a look.)

Can you think of any better training for Tinker Bell? Burlesque dancer turned circus performer? In her nightly act signaling the start of the fireworks, the ninety-pound, four-foot-ten pixie slid down a wire running from the Matterhorn to Sleeping Beauty Castle, as much as 146 feet above Disneyland's guests.[4] She performed the routine six nights a week for three summers, retiring from the act because of health problems. Can you blame her? The twenty-two-second flight path looked pretty smooth, but every night Tiny/Tink made a rather inglorious landing smashing into a full-sized mattress held in place by two brawny cast members. (And this, before pillow tops. Oh, Tink.) The fireworks show was plussed while Tiny got concussed. She once said, "I have no age in the air—but when my feet hit the ground I grow old."[5] Count me among her fans. Intrepid, spirited, and ageless—Tiny knew how to light up the sky.

P.S. Tink still sets off sparks in the night sky. If you're interested in the role, you need to be about five feet tall and under ninety-five pounds. As Tink, you'll be outfitted with a costume and battery pack weighing about fifty pounds.[6] At Disney World Tink climbs a ladder from the Cinderella Suite level to reach the high point of a zip line. There, safely attached to a harness, Tinker Bell is launched down the zip line with a good heave-ho of a fellow cast member. See, it's still okay and a grand adventure (if potentially hazardous) to be Tink!

HAPPILY EVER AFTER
It's Never Too Late

"Now it's time to say goodbye to all our family. . . ."[1] If you grew up watching *The Mickey Mouse Club* (or, like me, its reruns) you are probably humming along with the melody of this closing song made famous by the Mouseketeers. In my experience, singing those words can be easier than living them. I doubt we are ever really ready to say goodbye to the treasured people, places, and moments in our lives. But I will tell you that for all I learned in my thirty years at Disney, what I learned in the process of *leaving* Disney was every bit as valuable.

A friend asked me, "How do you know it's time to go?" My answer? Sometimes circumstances dictate it. Sometimes people tell you. For the most part, though, deep within, you know it's time to live a new adventure. And I recommend leaving before you're completely ready, so that whether it's a day at the park or a thirty-year career, the luster of your experience is never scuffed by exhaustion, regret, or other negativity. That said, I've found that no matter the circumstances, even when you know it's time, parting is a particularly sweet sorrow.

Transition

What happens after the parting is the space I call "the middle," or when I say I am "on the move." I have also heard it called "the hallway." This transition, the time in the middle, is a mixed bag of emotions (trail mix, for sure). It is equal parts excitement for what lies ahead, trepidation for the unknown, and usually a little sadness for what you leave behind. And while some transitions are blinking markers in our lives, we actually transition constantly and often quietly throughout our lives. We're always changing something—adding a commitment to our calendar, dropping a habit, taking a job, switching a route, saying goodbye to one school year and hello to the next. Some of these changes are barely noticed, a blip on our screen. Because of that, we can forget that newness in life most often comes by way of closure and, therefore, loss. The child who learns to walk never returns to crawling. The sister who marries is no longer your ever-available travel partner. The great job you landed means your routine of grabbing a quick soda with your favorite officemate has ended. It may help to remember that all change—even good change, involves loss. And every loss should be grieved.

So how do we cope with all that change, celebrating what's new while grieving what's lost? How do we manage transitions, the big and the daily, the sad and the delightful changes alike? Oh, I wish I knew! But I do have a few thoughts on those truly magical transitional times that we live through:

*P*eek back, but only peek. We should expect some sadness and nostalgic feelings in the midst of change. The very word *nostalgia* means a sickness for home, a longing for all that was familiar and that which no longer exists. Expect it, embrace it, and savor what was, all the while moving ahead. I have a framed piece that my friend, rescuer, and rock, Liz gave me when my sister Fifi and her husband moved across the country with "my" babies. (Sadness doesn't come close to describing how bereft I felt.) It reads: Don't cry because it's over. Smile because it happened. Know that it will take time to adjust, but try to smile at the memory. Appreciate that much of what you love about your past travels with you because your past shapes you for this time, this moment. Cherish those moments as you glance back, but don't do more than glance. The rearview mirror is smaller than the windshield for a reason.

Perspective is everything. Changing perspective is the greatest gift of your time "on the move." I spent thirty years looking at life through the lens of The Walt Disney Company. Now don't get me wrong, I wouldn't have traded one minute of those thirty years. (Okay, there may have been a few minutes I could have done without.) But when I left, I discovered something fabulous. Even though much of my life was interwoven with Mickey Mouse and company, Disney didn't define me. Jody was still Jody. This time taught me that my identity is not about performance, vocation, or fulfilling my dreams. True, life-giving identity is a gift from God—and a lifelong adventure.

No question, life without my Disney name tag was awkward in the beginning. I remember my first post-Disney function. The host asked everyone to introduce themselves and provide a little background information. I was still unprepared at my turn. I stumbled through my story like an idiot who didn't know what planet she was from: "Hi, I am Jody from . . . uh . . . um . . .

ah . . . from . . . well, the Dreyers." And then I smiled, so proud that I'd come up with my own last name. What a first impression I must have made! It took time, but eventually I found freedom in being Jody from wherever and whatever I wanted. Suddenly I had a new perspective. I was wearing a new lens to see the world.

*P*ossibilities abound with an expectant heart. Take full advantage of any new freedom you get in the gap. Explore, discover, and find new outlets for your interests and passions. You may even discover new purpose. Enjoy the transition with lots of curiosity and maybe greater availability. Think about new career options, take a class, or teach a class. Turn your passion into a paycheck (if even a small one). Make a new friend or visit an old one, go someplace you've always wanted to go—because you can. For me, transition is a mind-set, a gift. Transitions invite me to live with an expectant heart, anticipating the next adventure and walking into the future with faith that tells me no matter what lies ahead, God is already there.

Today

I read a Harvard University study that reported 47 percent of our waking hours are spent thinking about something that isn't going on. In case you just missed that (due to the truth of said factoid), let me repeat it: for roughly half of our awake time, our wandering minds are focused on something other than the present.[2] How can that be?

Overly wrapped up in the past or concerned about the future, we tend to overlook the present. Staying present, 100 percent, is a habit of intentionality, and I admit having to work at it. I am inspired by Mother Teresa's words: "The future is so much in the hands of God, I find it much more easy to accept today because yesterday is gone, tomorrow has not yet come, and we have only today. Let us begin."[3] I try not to regret the past or worry about what's to come. Besides, I've learned I don't usually stress about the right things anyway. So, as best I can, I kiss regret goodbye and let my faith be bigger than my fear.

Rabbits and Easter Eggs

Another part of staying present means I don't chase as many rabbits as I used to. And that means. . . . what exactly? Let's go back to the farm one last time and review the nature of rabbits. They are fast and nearly impossible to catch. The stinkers will make a game of eluding you, but they aren't going to lead you anywhere, except down a rabbit hole. (And that's where they'll leave you, breathless and frustrated.) And rabbits have a tendency to multiply. Chase one, and you're likely to find yourself chasing six. In life and in business, there are opportunities and there are rabbits. Beware of chasing rabbits. Instead, focus on the gift of today. If you focus on today and live in the present, you may find something more rewarding than a rabbit. You may find an Easter egg or two.

Disney and Pixar filmmakers frequently place visual surprises like three-circle silhouettes of Mickey Mouse and other images or text as a secret nod to other films, characters, and the shared traditions of the filmmakers. Finding these Easter eggs, also called Hidden Mickeys, has become a regular pursuit of many a

Disney fan. From bubbles in the shape of Mickey in *Snow White*, to Goofy and Donald Duck appearing in the undersea concert auditorium with King Triton in *The Little Mermaid*, to the poster of Mulan in Nani's room in *Lilo and Stitch*, Disney and Pixar animators wink at the audience and pay tribute to what has come before in almost every film.

What has been always influences what will be. In the same way, if you take the time to search, you will find hidden gems and winks from God in your own story. What forgotten acquaintance has reentered your story? What skill acquired long ago has suddenly become relevant and useful? What experience has uniquely prepared you for the journey you are on today? As is always the case, if you look too longingly on the past, you miss the moment that becomes tomorrow's treasure.

Don't miss today—even in the midst of transition. Because today, this very moment, is worth your full attention, and tomorrow's treasures are discovered today.

DEAR CASTLE FRIENDS

We can't thank you enough for taking this wild ride with us, and we hope you've felt a kinship with us in the journey. Like us, you may have a great love for all things Disney. For thirty years, Disney was my life. More accurately, it represented what I knew to be the best about life—the stuff that makes your heart beat faster and the hair on the back of your neck stand straight—the idea that life can be a great surprise, beyond the furthest reaches of our imagination. I think Walt Disney wanted to take us there—where life is adventure and goodness is celebrated.

Disney led me as a young girl to once upon a time, to the land of fairy tales and imagination. As an adult, I have come to believe that one fairy tale in particular is true for all time, in my world and yours. Frederick Buechner put it this way: "It is a world of magic and mystery, of deep darkness and flickering starlight. It is a world where terrible things happen and wonderful things too. . . . Yet for all its confusion and wildness, it is a world where the battle goes ultimately to the good, who live happily ever after, and where in the long run everybody, good and evil alike, becomes known by his true name."[1]

Our hope is that this book will help you sort through everything from who you are, at the core, to the complicated characters in your life and the times and places you've been stuck, as well as those occasions that demand fireworks! Our greater hope is that *Beyond the Castle* becomes a gateway to a deeper appreciation for the fairy tale that is your story and to the happily ever after that God offers to us all. That's the adventure that matters, and the one that leads us to happily *every* after: day after every day, year after every year.

Castle friends, your ride awaits. Go! *Enjoy* the journey. We wish you every blessing as you live your own happily ever after.

With love and affection, and a ginormous hug
—*Jody (and Stacy)*

TAKE A BOW

* Our moms and dads, our first and best tour guides who encouraged us to believe that, indeed, life could be magical . . .
* John Dreyer and Jeff, our supportive, loving, rock-solid partners . . .
* Matt, Haley, and all of our precious babies young and old . . .
* Our cast of characters (family and friends) with us every step of the way . . .
* Our Young Life family (shout out to Terry Swenson and Josh Griffin)
* SUPER STAR Support: Kase Waddell, Val Cohen, Lila McGinnis, Gary Buchanan, Annette Bourland, Karol Carbiener, Cherain and Marc Smith, friends at the Smokehouse Restaurant, and the Friday Writers and Walkers
* From beginning to end: Jill Owston (aka sister Fifi)
* Editors Extraordinaire: Nancy Erickson (our very own PhD book doctor), Carolyn McCready (got us off to a great start), and Kim Tanner (always photo ready) . . .
* Amazing Alicia Kasen, Jennifer get-the-word-out VerHage, and the awesome Z team . . .
* David Morris for believing in us and *Beyond* . . .
* The entire HarperCollins Christian Publishing Family!

Because of all of you, our dreams keep coming true.
You have blessed us and we are grateful.

NOTES

Chapter 1: Vacations

1. Jeff Kurtti, *Disneyland—From Once upon a Time to Happily Ever After* (New York: Disney Editions, 2010), 5.
2. Disney Book Group, *The Quotable Walt Disney* (New York: Disney Editions Delux, 2001), 262.

Chapter 2: Tiaras

1. "A Challenge to Barbie: Can a Disney Princess Topple the Queen of Toyland?" *The Economist*, April 17, 2003, www.theeconomist.com/node/1719558.
2. Eliza Berman, "Why Disney Decided to Make Moana the Ultimate Anti-Princess," September 2, 2016, http://time.com/4473277/moana-disney-princess-directors-interview/.
3. Clifton StrengthsFinder®, www.gallupstrengthscenter.com.
4. Frederick Buechner, *Wishful Thinking: A Seeker's ABC* (New York: HarperOne, 1993), 118–19.
5. Mary Tomlinson, "On-Purpose Partners," www.MaryTomlinson.com.
6. *The Quotable Walt Disney*, 85.
7. Laura Michelle Kelly and Gavin Lee, vocal performance of "Jolly Holiday," recorded May 8, 2007, on *Mary Poppins Original London Cast Recording*, Walt Disney Records, compact disc.
8. Diane Disney Miller, "My Dad, Walt Disney: Part 6," *Saturday Evening Post* (1956). Also available one, http://www.saturdayeveningpost.com/wp-content/uploads/satevepost/Disneys-Folly1.pdf.
9. *The Quotable Walt Disney*, 105.

Chapter 3: What's Inside

1. Jim Fanning, *The Disney Book: A Celebration of the World of Disney* (New York: DK, 2015), 103.
2. Jérémie Noyer, "*Beauty and the Beast*: Glen Keane on Discovering the Beauty in the Beast," http://animatedviews.com/2010/beauty-and-the-beast-glen-keane-on-discovering-the-beauty-in-the-beast/.

3. Kevin Lane Keller, "The Brand Report Card," https://hbr.org/2000/01/the
-brand-report-card.

4. Billy Stanek, "Dateline Disney 1985," *Disney Newsreel*, January 15, 2010.

5. "The Walt Disney Company (US)," http://www.adbrands.net/us/disney_us.htm.

6. Brady Willett and Todd Alway, "The Walt Disney Company," 2003, http://
www.fallstreet.com/disney-dis.pdf.

7. "Stanley Gold and Roy Disney Statements at Annual Meeting of Walt Disney
Co.," March 3, 2004, http://www.prnewswire.com/news-releases/stanley-gold
-and-roy-disney-statements-at-annual-meeting-of-walt-disney-co-march-3
-2004-58781897.html.

8. Ibid.

9. Jensen, Michael C. "Integrity: Without It Nothing Works," *Rotman Magazine*,
April 6, 2014, 16–20. Also available online, http://ssrn.com/abstract=1511274.

10. Noyer, http://animatedviews.com/2010/beauty-and-the-beast-glen-keane-on
-discovering-the-beauty-in-the-beast/.

11. *The Quotable Walt Disney*, 139.

Chapter 4: Story

1. *Disney Institute Custom Solutions Guidebook* (Disney Book Group).

2. "Attention Span Statistics," 2016, http://www.statisticbrain.com/attention
-span-statistics.

3. "The Lion King," 1994, www.lionking.org/text/FilmNotes.html.

4. Phil Mooney, "Bite the Wax Tadpole?" http://www.coca-colacompany.com/
stories/bite-the-wax-ta.

5. Blaise Pascal, "Of the Means of Belief," http://www.bartleby.com/48/1/4.html.

6. Chuck Schmidt, "Covering Disneyland for L.A. Paper Helped Charlie
Ridgway Launch His Legendary Career with Disney," http://blog.silive.com/
goofy_about_disney/2014/01/post_29.html (2014).

7. Jonathan D. Leavitt and Nicholas J. S. Christenfeld, "The fluency of spoilers:
Why giving away endings improves stories," http://psy2.ucsd.edu/~nchristenfeld/
Publications_files/Fluency%20of%20Spoilers.pdf, 94.

8. John Wooden and Steve Jamison, *The Essential Wooden: A Lifetime of
Lessons on Leaders and Leadership* (New York: McGraw-Hill, 2007), 13.

9. Brené Brown, *The Gifts of Imperfection: Let Go of Who You Think You're
Supposed to Be and Embrace Who You Are* (Center City, MN: Hazeldon
Publishing, 2016), 6.

10. *The Lion King: DVD Two-Disc Platinum Edition*, Walt Disney Video, 2003.

Chapter 5: Characters

1. *The Quotable Walt Disney*, 95.

2. Ibid., 40.
3. Jen Hatmaker, *For the Love: Fighting for Grace in a World of Impossible Standards* (Nashville: Thomas Nelson, 2015), 134.
4. Wayde Goodall, *Success Kills: Sidestep the Snares That Will Steal Your Dreams* (Green Forest, AZ: New Leaf Press, 2009), 49.

Chapter 6: Castle Guests

1. Judith Rubin, ed., *TEA/AECOM 2016 Theme Index and Museum Index: The Global Attractions Attendance Report* (Themed Entertainment Association, 2016), 9.
2. Bob Thomas, *Walt Disney: An American Original* (New York: Disney Editions, 1994), 288.
3. The Disney Institute, with Theodore Kinni, *Be Our Guest: Perfecting the Art of Customer Service* (New York: Disney Editions, 2001), 42.
4. https://www.brainyquote.com/quotes/quotes/p/peterdruck134881.html.
5. Allen Adamson, contributor, "Disney Knows It's Not Just Magic That Keeps a Brand on Top," 2014, http://www.forbes.com/sites/allenadamson/2014/10/15/disney-knows-its-not-just-magic-that-keeps-a-brand-on-top/#7f79e0db44ff.

Chapter 7: Go Team!

1. *The Quotable Walt Disney*, 96.
2. Hatmaker, 197.
3. Michael D. Eisner with Tony Schwartz, *Work in Progress: Risking Failure, Surviving Success* (New York: Hyperion, 1999), 237.
4. http://articles.courant.com/2000-02-25/sports/0002250078_1_new-englanders-miracle-locker-room.
5. Erin Stough, "Fantasound: How Disney Brought Stereophonic Sound to the Big Screen," November 2015, http://www.laughingplace.com/w/articles/2015/11/19/fantasound-how-disney-brought-stereophonic-sound-to-the-big-screen/.

Chapter 8: Who Knew?

1. From the estate of Dr. Martin Luther King Jr., http://old.seattletimes.com/special/mlk/king/words/blueprint.html.
2. *The Quotable Walt Disney*, 90.

Chapter 9: Enjoy the Ride

1. Julia Fawal, 2015, http://www.womansday.com/life/travel-tips/a51303/10-things-you-never-knew-about-roller-coasters/.
2. Kevin DeYoung, *Just Do Something: A Liberating Approach to Finding God's Will* (Chicago: Moody, 2009), 35.

3. Ibid., 13.

4. http://www.slate.com/articles/business/operations/2012/06/queuing_theory _what_people_hate_most_about_waiting_in_line_.html.

5. Andee Olson, "Why *Fixer Upper's* Chip and Joanna Gaines Are the Best Real Life Couple on TV," 2016, http://www.vogue.com/13405685/fixer-upper-chip -joanna-gaines-magnolia-hgtv/.

6. Oliver Smith, "The Channel Tunnel: 20 Fascinating Facts," 2015, http://www. telegraph.co.uk/travel/destinations/europe/france/articles/The-Channel-Tunnel -20-fascinating-facts/.

7. Joshua Barajas, "8 Things You Didn't Know about Dr. Seuss," 2015, http:// www.pbs.org/newshour/art/8-things-didnt-know-dr-seuss/.

8. Theodore S. Geisel and Audrey S. Geisel, *Oh, The Places You'll Go!* (New York: Random House, 1990), n.p.

9. HDThrillSeeker, comments on https://www.youtube.com/watch?v=hSoAd8qgGSQ.

Chapter 10: Stuck

1. *The Quotable Walt Disney*, 107.

2. Ibid., 106.

3. Lou Mongelle, "Walt Disney World History 101—'How to Buy 27,000 Acres of Land and Have No One Notice," 2005, http://www.wdwradio.com/2005/ 02/wdw-history-101-how-to-buy-27000-acres-of-land-and-no-one-noticeq/.

4. Herb Leibacher, "Six Fascinating Facts about Walt's Airplane on Display at Disney's Hollywood Studios," March 3, 2014, https://www.worldofwalt.com/ fascinating-facts-walts-airplane-disneys-hollywood-studios.html.

5. Jack Williams, "How Things Work: Lightning Protection," 2011, http:// www.airspacemag.com/flight-today/how-things-work-lightning-protection -161993347/?no-ist.

6. @timkellernyc, https://twitter.com/timkellernyc/status/420953309701480448.

Chapter 11: Open Hands

1. Matthew Alice, "Why Does Mickey Mouse Only Have Three fingers?" 2001, http://www.sandiegoreader.com/news/2001/nov/29/why-does-mickey-mouse -only-have-three-fingers/.

2. Andrew Berrington, "Palm Sunday 1965: Southern Great Lakes Ravaged by One of the Worst Tornado Outbreaks on Record," 2015, http://www.us tornadoes.com/2015/04/11/palm-sunday-1965-southern-great-lakes-ravaged -by-one-of-the-worst-tornado-outbreaks-on-record/.

3. The story can be found in Matthew 14:13–21.

4. "The Most Fun You Can Have with Money," http://www.daveramsey.com/ blog/most-fun-you-can-have-with-money.

5. https://ditm-twdc-us.storage.googleapis.com/2015/11/Disney_30Year _Infographic_7.pdf.

6. Ralph Waldo Emerson, *The Complete Works of Ralph Waldo Emerson: Essays*, 2nd Series, vol. 3 (New York: Houghton, Mifflin, 1903–1904), 323.

7. "2013 Walt Disney Legacy Award Recipients Announced," https://public affairs.disneyland.com/2013-walt-disney-legacy-award-recipients-announced/.

Chapter 12: Fireworks

1. "Firework," http://www.dictionary.com/browse/firework.

2. "Precision Fireworks Display System Having a Decreased Environmental Impact," 1994, http://www.google.com/patents/US5339741; http://disney auditions.com/other-opportunities/.

3. "2013 Walt Disney Legacy Award Recipients Announced."

4. Tiny Kline, ed. by Janet M. Davis *Circus Queen & Tinker Bell: The Memoir of Tiny Kline* (Chicago: University of Illinois Press, 2008).

5. "Pepito the Clown Mentioned in Tiny Kline's Memoir (1917)," http://www .pepitoandjoanne.com/Blog/Entries/1917/11/1_Pepito_the_Clown_Mentioned _in_Tiny_Klines_Memoir_(1917).html.

6. "Tinker Bell Takes Flight in Magic Kingdom's New Show 'Wishes," 2012, http://www.bestoforlando.com/articles/tinker-bell-takes-flight-in-magic -kingdoms-new-show-wishes/.

Happily Ever After

1. Jimmie Dodd, "Mickey Mouse March," Hal Leonard Corporation, 1955.

2. Steve Bradt, "Wandering Mind Not a Happy Mind," 2010, http://news .harvard.edu/gazette/story/2010/11/wandering-mind-not-a-happy-mind/.

3. Mother Teresa, ed. Brian Kolodiejchuk, *Where There Is Love, There Is God: A Path to Closer Union with God and Greater Love for Others* (New York: Doubleday Religion, 2010), 191.

Dear Castle Friends

1. Frederick Buechner, *Telling the Truth: The Gospel as Tragedy, Comedy, and Fairy Tale* (New York: Harper, 1977), 81.